The Way Out
and
The Way In

Studies in Exodus and Leviticus
R.E. Harlow

Everyday Publications
310 Killaly St. W.
Port Colborne, ON, Canada L3K 6A6

The Way Out of Egypt

NEW LIFE MINISTRY
(Head Office)
P.O. Box 123
Arva, Ont. N0M 1C0

The Way Into the Holiest

Seventh Impression 1992

ISBN 0-919586-01-5

Printed in Canada

READ THIS !

There may be a thousand books about Exodus and Leviticus in the English language. Our plan has been to explain the meaning of these Bible books in simple language. We hope that this will be a help to new readers of the Bible.

Both Exodus and Leviticus are very important books. If you know the teaching of Exodus and Leviticus you will be able to understand better many other parts of the Bible. You will also know more about God.

We would also like to thank Mr. Reynold L. Woodward who drew the pictures of the tabernacle.

R. E. Harlow

READ THE BIBLE EVERY DAY

Day	First Month	Second Month	Third Month
1	Ex. 1. 1–14	13. 1–10	25. 1– 9
2	1.15–22	13.11–22	25.10–22
3	2. 1–10	14. 1–18	25.23–30
4	2.11–25	14.19–31	25.31–40
5	3. 1– 6	15. 1–12	26. 1–10
6	3. 7–13	15.13–18	26.11–25
7	3.14–22	15.19–27	26.26–37
8	4. 1– 9	16. 1– 8	27. 1– 8
9	4.10–20	16. 9–21	27. 9–21
10	4.21–31	16.22–36	28. 1–14
11	5. 1– 9	17. 1– 7	28.15–30
12	5.10–23	17. 8–16	28.31–43
13	6. 1–13	18. 1–12	29. 1–14
14	6.14–27	18.13–27	29.15–25
15	6.28–7.13	19. 1–15	29.26–34
16	7.14–24	19.16–25	29.35–46
17	7.25–8.15	20. 1– 6	30. 1–10
18	8.16–32	20. 7–16	30.11–21
19	9. 1–12	20.17–26	30.22–38
20	9.13–26	21. 1–11	31. 1–11
21	9.27–35	21.12–25	31.12–18
22	10. 1–11	21.26–36	32. 1–10
23	10.12–20	22. 1– 9	32.11–24
24	10.21–29	22.10–20	32.25–35
25	11. 1–10	22.21–31	33. 1–11
26	12. 1–13	23. 1–11	33.12–23
27	12.14–20	23.12–22	34. 1–10
28	12.21–27	23.23–33	34.11–24
29	12.28–39	24. 1– 8	34.25–35
30	12.40–51	24. 9–18	35. 1– 9

READ THE BIBLE EVERY DAY

Day	Fourth Month	Fifth Month	Sixth Month
1	35.10–29	7.11–21	17. 1– 9
2	35.30–36.1	7.22–38	17.10–16
3	36. 2–13	8. 1–13	18. 1–18
4	36.14–30	8.14–29	18.19–30
5	36.31–38	8.30–36	19. 1–12
6	37. 1–16	9. 1–11	19.13–25
7	37.17–29	9.12–24	19.26–37
8	38. 1– 8	10. 1–11	20. 1–16
9	38. 9–23	10.12–20	20.17–27
10	38.24–31	11. 1–12	21. 1–15
11	39. 1– 7	11.13–28	21.16–24
12	39. 8–26	11.29–38	22. 1– 9
13	39.27–43	11.39–47	22.10–25
14	40. 1–15	12. 1– 8	22.26–33
15	40.16–33	13. 1– 8	23. 1– 8
16	40.34–38	13. 9–23	23. 9–14
17	Lev. 1. 1– 9	13.24–37	23.15–25
18	1.10–17	13.38–46	23.26–36
19	2. 1–10	13.47–59	23.37–44
20	2.11–16	14. 1– 9	24. 1– 9
21	3. 1–11	14.10–20	24.10–23
22	3.12–17	14.21–32	25. 1–12
23	4. 1–12	14.33–42	25.13–24
24	4.13–26	14.43–57	25.25–38
25	4.27–36	15. 1–12	25.39–55
26	5. 1–10	15.13–24	26. 1–13
27	5.11–19	15.25–33	26.14–33
28	6. 1–13	16. 1–10	26.34–46
29	6.14–30	16.11–22	27. 1–15
30	7. 1–10	16.23–34	27.16–34

THE BOOK OF EXODUS

EXODUS

Lesson 1
GOD CALLED MOSES, chapters 1-4.

In Genesis we see the beginning of the human race, chapters 1-11, and the beginning of the chosen race, Israel, chapters 12-50. God called Abraham out from among the Gentile nations and gave him some great promises. He told Abraham that he would be the father of a nation and after a while the land of promise would belong to his descendants. Abraham's family grew until his son's son, Jacob, had twelve sons, but they were still strangers in the land of promise. One of them, Joseph, became ruler in Egypt and provided food for the chosen nation in time of hunger. Genesis ends when Jacob died in Egypt.

The book of Exodus goes on with the story of the chosen people. A new king in Egypt made them slaves. Exodus tells how God led His people out of Egypt into the desert. The word Exodus means *"the way out"*. We will study the book of Exodus in eight lessons:

Exodus was written by Moses, 17.14; 34.27. When the Lord Jesus Christ was teaching about Exodus 20, He said that Moses had spoken these words, Mark 7.10.

In the first twelve chapters the people of Israel are in **Egypt**, slaves of Pharaoh. God delivered them and in chapters 13-18 they are seen in the **desert**. In the rest of the book, chapters 19-40, they are at **Mount Sinai**. There they received the Law of God through Moses. They also learned how to build the tabernacle.

The people of Israel were slaves, chapter 1.

Seventy people entered Egypt and the names of Jacob's sons are listed here, vs.1-4, as they were in Genesis 46.8-27. Joseph died

7

in Egypt at the age of 110 years, but we do not know when or where the other brothers died. Moses was born about sixty years after Joseph had died.

Foreign kings ruled in Egypt in the time of Joseph. These kings were descendants of Shem, the son of Noah, but the Egyptians were the descendants of Ham. This may be one reason why the king of Egypt was friendly to Joseph who also was a Shemite. Soon after Joseph died, the Egyptian people destroyed the foreign kings and put an Egyptian back on the throne. *"There arose a new king over Egypt, who did not know Joseph,"* v.8. Israel had become a great nation and this new king was afraid of their power. He feared that they would join with the enemies of Egypt and help overthrow the country. To keep the people of Israel from getting any richer he made them work without pay. Pharaoh set masters over the men of Israel and they made them build two cities for Pharaoh, v.11. In spite of this hard work the nation of Israel grew larger and larger, v.12.

Then the king of Egypt decided that all Hebrew baby boys must be destroyed. He called the women who helped the mothers of Israel and told them to kill every baby boy when he was born. The women would not obey the king in this. They said that the Hebrew babies were born quickly before they could come to help the mothers. So Pharaoh commanded the men of Egypt to destroy every baby boy born to the people of Israel.

It might seem that the women told Pharaoh a lie in verse 19. If they did, we can be sure that God would not bless them for telling lies. We know from many other parts of the Bible that God hates lying, Revelation 21.8,27.

Israel in Egypt is a picture of people who are slaves of Satan. The life of the Israelites was unhappy because of the hard work they had to do, v.14. They had no way of escape. However God was still with His people and soon started to deliver them.

Moses was born and educated, chapter 2.

Chapter 2 tells how God began to prepare a deliverer for His people Israel. He chose the tribe of Levi, the third son of Jacob. Levi (with his brother Simeon) had cruelly killed the men of Shechem, Genesis 34.25. Levi seemed to be no better than his brothers and Jacob gave no special blessing to him, Genesis 49.5.

God often chooses weak men to put to shame those who are strong, 1 Corinthians 1.27. To deliver Israel God did not choose anyone from the tribes of Reuben or Judah or Joseph. Those who are strong may trust too much in their own strength. When God uses a man in His service, **God** must get all the glory. God can use anyone who is willing for God to use him.

The name of Moses' father was Amram and his mother's name was Jochebed, 6.20. Moses' brother Aaron was three years older than Moses, 7.7. When Moses was born, his father and mother saw that he was a beautiful child. By faith they hid him for three months. They were not afraid of the king's command, Hebrews 11.23.

The king had commanded that every baby should be put into the river, 1.22. Moses' father and mother *did* put him into the river, but Moses was saved from death by a little boat made of grasses. This basket was covered with a black material which kept the water out.

Like the great ark of Noah 772 years before this little boat is a picture of the Lord Jesus Christ. The result of breaking God's Law is death. The Law of God cannot be set aside, but Christ came in to save us from death. God did not change His Law. The Lord Jesus Christ took the full judgment of our sins on Himself, 1 Peter 2.24.

When Moses' mother put him in the river, she left his sister Miriam to look after him, vs.4-10. The king's daughter came down to wash at the river with her maidens. When she saw the baby and heard him cry she had pity on him. The king's daughter told Miriam to go and call a nurse to look after the baby. Miriam went and called her own mother. The king's daughter took the baby as her own. She called him **Moses** because she drew him out of the water.

No doubt Moses' mother taught him to fear Jehovah and told him about the great men of Genesis. When he was older he was educated as a prince of Egypt, Acts 7.21,22. It would seem that neither Pharaoh nor his daughter had any sons of their own. Pharaoh's daughter was training Moses to be the next king. When Moses grew up he refused to be called the son of Pharaoh's daughter. He chose to suffer with God's people rather than to enjoy the life of a prince in Egypt, Hebrews 11.24-26. Moses knew that Joseph long before had been able to help his own people when he became the second ruler of Egypt. Moses might have thought that **he** should become king so he could do the same. Instead he chose to be separated from the Egyptians and to belong to the people of Israel. This was the right thing to do and God honoured Moses for deciding in this way. Today millions of people know who Moses was. Very few even know the name of the Pharaoh who ruled in Egypt at that time.

However Moses had many lessons to learn. When he was 40 years old he went to visit the people of Israel and tried to help them. Moses defended one of his brothers against an Egyptian and killed the Egyptian, vs.11-15. The next day he tried to stop two men of Israel from fighting. He thought that his brothers would understand that God would deliver them through him. Instead of that they rejected him and said, *"Who made you a ruler and a judge over us?"* Acts 7.23-28.

Moses' reasons were good and he knew that God was calling him. However Moses did not wait for the right time and he did not do things in the right way. It was not yet God's time to lead Israel out of Egypt and certainly Moses should not have gone in the way of Cain by killing a man. Moses was afraid when he knew that others had seen him kill the man. Pharaoh tried to kill Moses and Moses ran away. Even this was a sign of Moses' faith because he knew that God had called him. *"By faith he left Egypt, not being afraid of the anger of the king"*, Hebrews 11.27. His real desire was to keep his eyes on the Lord and wait until God's time would come.

Moses ran away to the land of Midian, vs.15-22. Midian was a son of Abraham and his wife Keturah, Genesis 25.2. Reuel, the priest of Midian was also called Jethro, 3.1. He had seven daughters who looked after his sheep. Moses sat down beside the well and saw these daughters draw water for their father's sheep. The other shepherds drove Reuel's daughters away but Moses stood up to help them. Moses was always trying to help other people. Later God used Moses' desire to help others and sent him to save the people of Israel.

The priest of Midian wanted Moses to live with him. He gave him Zipporah his daughter as his wife. Remember that Isaac and Jacob each got his wife at a well of water, Genesis 24.11; 29.2. When Moses' wife had a baby, Moses called his name Gershom.

God knew that His people were having great trouble in Egypt, vs.23-25. He was preparing His servant Moses to deliver them, but it was not yet God's time.

The call of Moses, chapters 3,4.

We can divide the life of Moses into three parts of 40 years each. He was 40 years in Egypt in Pharaoh's house. There he learned all the wisdom of the Egyptians. Then he spent 40 years

10

in the desert. There he was learning in the school of God and God's wisdom is very different from men's. David, another great man of God, learned the ways of God as he looked after his father's sheep under the starry heavens. Paul after he turned to Christ went to the desert of Arabia for a while, Galatians 1.17. After 80 years of training Moses was ready for his life work. During the last 40 years of his life he delivered Israel from Egypt and brought them to the edge of the Promised Land, Acts 7.22,23,30, Deuteronomy 34.7.

Every child of God is in God's school. He is teaching us His lessons every day. As we learn in the presence of God we will be able to go out and serve Him.

When God called Moses, he was working with his hands, looking after Jethro's sheep. Moses journeyed on looking for grass for the sheep and came to Mount Horeb. This is also called Mount Sinai. Years later at this very place Moses received the Law of God, 19.20, Numbers 10.12, Deuteronomy 1.6.

When God called David he was looking after his father's sheep, 1 Samuel 16.11-13. God called Elisha while he was working in a field, 1 Kings 19.19-21. Peter and Andrew, James and John were busy fishing or getting ready to fish, Mark 1.16-20. The Lord called them to follow Him. It is important for a Christian to work with his hands, 1 Thessalonians 4.10-12.

In Mount Horeb the Angel of the Lord appeared to Moses in a flame of fire. Who is this Angel of Jehovah? The word angel means messenger and the angels are spirits whom God created to serve Him. In the book of Genesis *"the Angel of the Lord"* is used of God Himself, Genesis 16.11,13; 22.11-18. No man can look at God, but we can look at the Son of God, John 1.18. *"The Angel of the Lord"* is the Son of God. The Son was to become the Saviour of the world. In this chapter He was very much interested in delivering Israel from Egypt. Moses became a picture of the Lord Jesus Christ and the deliverance from Egypt is a picture of our salvation, Isaiah 63.9.

Sometimes God appeared as a man, Genesis 18.1,2. Here in Exodus 2 He appeared in fire, Hebrews 12.29. The little tree looked as if it were burning, but it was not destroyed! Moses knew that there was something wonderful about this. Only God could keep the tree from burning up, so Moses knew that God must be near. He was ready for a message from Jehovah. Moses was standing on holy ground and the Lord told him to take off his shoes. The ground had been cursed because of Adam's sin, Genesis 3.17, but God by His grace can change a curse into a blessing. Indeed this is what He loves to do.

Then God told Moses that He was the God of Amram, Moses' father, and the God of Abraham, Isaac and Jacob, v.6. Moses had taken off his shoes but now he hid his face from the sight of God. The Lord Jesus Christ used this verse to prove that men rise from the dead. God is not the God of dead men, but of living men, Matthew 22.32.

Jehovah kept on speaking, vs.7-10. He told Moses that He had seen the troubles of Israel and heard their cry. He had come down to deliver His people from Egypt. He commanded Moses to go back to Pharaoh for this purpose. Notice these words:

I am — verse 6
I have seen — verse 7
I have come down — verse 8
I will send you — verse 10

The Angel of Jehovah, the Son of God, felt sorry for His people Israel. He wanted to bring them out of slavery and into a good land, v.8. When He was in this world the Lord Jesus saw people as sheep without a shepherd and felt sorry for them. He told His disciples to pray that the Lord would send out workers. Then He sent **them** out to preach the Gospel, Matthew 9.36-10.1. He said to Moses *"I am God.....I will send* **you.**" Now in heaven the Lord Jesus still knows the sorrows of men who are slaves of sin. He is still sorry for them and is still sending His servants to tell others the way of salvation. He says *"All authority....has been given to me. Go therefore,"* Matthew 28.18,19. Every Christian should be helping in the work of the Lord. The Lord may call some to give all their time to His work. Until then we should keep busy working with our hands but waiting to hear His call, 1 Thessalonians 4.11.

Moses tried to refuse God's call, 3.11-4.17.

Today when God calls men, some try to refuse. They try to think of a good reason for not obeying God's command. Moses was no better. He tried to refuse God's call five times.

1. **His own littleness**, vs.11,12. Moses did not feel able to go to Pharaoh and ask him to let Israel go. Moses ran away from Pharaoh forty years before this because Pharaoh wanted to kill him. No doubt **that** king had died, but we can still understand why Moses would be afraid to go back. God's answer was that He would be

with Moses. He told Moses that he would lead Israel out of Egypt and they would serve God right there at Mount Horeb (Mount Sinai). This promise was a sign to faith alone because it would not be seen until after the promise had been fulfilled. Moses at that minute did not have that kind of faith.

We should be ready to serve the Lord and witness for Him before all men both small and great. If you feel afraid, remember that the Lord has promised *"I will be with you,"* v.12, Matthew 28.20.

2. **The ignorance of the people.** Moses felt that the people did not know God and this was partly true. He was really afraid that the people would not believe God had sent him. Moses knew that the One speaking to him was the God of Abraham, Isaac and Jacob, v.6. Moses' question is really just another attempt to refuse God's command. The Lord God has full authority to command His servants to do His will. Those who know the greatness of God must obey at once. Jehovah answered Moses by calling Himself "I AM WHO I AM", v.14. This wonderful name suggests that God is great enough in Himself. He had no beginning. He is the Uncreated One, the Eternal One.

These words also mean, *"I will become whatever I please."* This does not mean that God will change, but that He does not have to give account to anyone. God works out His own purposes according to His own counsel. This name also shows us that man cannot know God unless He reveals Himself, 1 Timothy 6.16, Romans 11.33-36.

When God revealed Himself as the **I AM** Moses could not answer and so God spoke again. He explained with great care what He was going to do and what He wanted Moses to do, vs.15-22.

(1) Israel would hear and accept the words of Moses, vs.15-18.

(2) Pharaoh would not listen to Moses' words, v.19.

(3) Later Pharaoh would be glad to let Israel go, vs.20-22.

(4) Moses should ask Pharaoh to let Israel go into the wilderness for three days' journey to sacrifice to God, v.18. God promised that He would help Moses against Pharaoh by giving him great powers, v.20. Israel would get paid for all the work they had done in Egypt, v.22.

3. Still Moses would not obey the Lord. He said, *"They will NOT believe me or listen to my voice,"* 4.1. By saying this he denied what the Lord had just promised in 3.18. It is a terrible thing to deny the word of God. God did not rebuke Moses at this time, but He gave him three signs. These signs would show the people of

13

Israel that the Lord had sent Moses.

(1) Moses' rod became a snake, then it became a rod again.

(2) Moses' hand became like a leper's, then was cleansed again.

(3) Water from the Nile river would become blood.

Later on when the people of Israel saw these signs they believed, 4.30,31, just as God had promised. Aaron used the first sign before Pharaoh, 7.10, and the third sign became the first of the ten blows which God dealt to Egypt, 7.17.

4. By now God had promised to be with Moses, had revealed His great name I AM and had given Moses these signs. Still Moses tried again to refuse. This time he said that he was not a good speaker. He never had been able to speak well in past years nor since Jehovah had been talking to him, v.10. The gifts which God gives grow when we use them. Moses became one of the greatest speakers the world has ever known. Before he died he gave to the people of Israel the great messages which are found in the book of Deuteronomy.

In answer to this the Lord told Moses that He was the Creator of man's mouth. He could give Moses the power to speak well. He can also make people so they cannot speak or hear or see. If we do not use the gift which God has given, we will lose it. The Lord Jesus Christ told the story of a king who gave one pound to each of his servants. One servant did not use his gift and so he lost it, Luke 19.24,26. If Moses refused to go and do God's will, he might become unable to speak at all.

5. Moses tried once more to refuse God's command. He said that God could send some other person, v.13. This made the Lord angry with Moses. He said that Moses' brother Aaron was a good speaker and he would go with Moses. Aaron did go with Moses, but he was certainly not a help to him at all times, for example 32.21.

When God called Moses, he tried to refuse, but God would not let him go. If Moses had finally refused to do God's will, God of course could have raised up somebody else. What a terrible loss this would have been to Moses himself! Be sure you are not refusing to do God's will for some little reason. God will make you give account for your life. He will punish us for not obeying.

Moses took the sheep back to Jethro and asked him if he could return to Egypt, vs.18-20. The Lord told Moses that his enemies in Egypt were dead. Moses took his family and the rod which he would use in Egypt to show God's power. On the way back the Lord spoke to him again and told him that he would have a terrible struggle with Pharaoh, vs.21-23.

Even before he got to Egypt, Moses had another problem. It seemed that his second son, Eliezer, 18.4, had not been circumcised. Circumcision was the sign of God's covenant with Abraham, Genesis 17.9-14. Every son of Abraham had to cut the flesh of his baby boys when they were eight days old. Moses could not expect victory over his enemies unless he obeyed the command of God. Zipporah did not like this even though her own father was a descendant of Abraham.

At this time God told Aaron to go and meet Moses at Mount Sinai, vs.27-31. When the two brothers reached Egypt, they called the people together. Moses and Aaron showed them the wonderful signs and told them what God was going to do. The people believed their words, as God had promised, 3.18, and they worshipped the Lord.

No one can expect to serve the Lord without obeying His commands. As soon as you understand a truth of Scripture, you should start to practise it. In this way God will lead you on to do greater things for Him.

15

Lesson 2
MOSES' STRUGGLE WITH PHARAOH, chapters 5-10.

When Moses was 80 years old, God called him to deliver His people from Egypt. After five attempts to refuse Moses finally obeyed God's command. He and Aaron came to the people of Israel and the people agreed that God had sent them.

The first demand to Pharaoh, chapter 5.

Moses and Aaron went in to Pharaoh. They told him that Jehovah wanted the Israelites to go into the wilderness and worship Him. Pharaoh asked, *"Who is Jehovah?"* and refused to let Israel go. It seems that the Israelites had not told the Egyptians very much about Jehovah. In fact they may have been worshipping the gods of Egypt. Just a little later they worshipped strange gods, Acts 7.42,43. Anyway Pharaoh considered himself to be equal to a god. He thought that the Israelites simply wanted to get out of work. He commanded Moses and Aaron to get on with **their** work like the other men of Israel. The result of this first demand was more work for Israel.

The Israelites made bricks to build the cities for Pharaoh. They needed dry grass to make bricks. Up to this time Pharaoh's servants had brought the dry grass. Now the people of Israel must get their own grass. Still they had to make just as many bricks as before. The masters kept urging the people to finish their work, vs.10-14.

The officers of Israel went to Pharaoh but he refused to listen to them, vs.15-21. Pharaoh told them that **they** were idle and for this reason they wanted to go and sacrifice to Jehovah. Then the officers met Moses and Aaron. They were afraid that Pharaoh would kill them and it would be Moses' and Aaron's fault.

Even Moses' faith became weak. He turned to the Lord and said that it was all **His** fault. The Lord encouraged him to believe, 5.22-6.1.

The Lord's reply, 6.2-7.7.

The Lord allows His people to get into trouble so that He can show His great power and love for them. By now the people of Israel were certainly in great trouble and so the Lord came to their help. First He promised that Pharaoh would not only let them go, he would force them to leave his land, 6.1.

In many Bibles the name LORD in four large letters means Jehovah. This wonderful Name is used of God as the One who makes a covenant with His people. Abraham knew this name of God, Ge-

16

nesis 15.7,8; 18.14. Now God is about to fulfil His covenant promise, Genesis 15.13-16, to act as Jehovah, vs.2-5. He told Moses just what to say to the people of Israel, vs.6-8. The first words in this message were *"I am the LORD"* and the last words were the same. God promised to deliver them from Egypt, to make them His people, and to bring them into a good land. Still the people would not listen, v.9.

Then the LORD told Moses to go again to Pharaoh, but Moses refused. His lips were no better than those of an uncircumcised man who did not know God. The people of Israel would not listen to him. Why go to Pharaoh? However the Lord told Moses and Aaron what to do, vs.10-13.

We find these words again in verses 28-30 and after that Moses and Aaron went to Pharaoh. First however we have a list of the names of the sons of Levi, vs.14-27. Levi was the third son of Jacob, so the sons of Reuben and Simeon his older brothers are given first, vs.14,15. Levi had three sons, Gershon, Kohath and Merari. Amram, the son of Kohath, married Jochebed his father's sister, v.20. (Later on God's law said that this was not right, Leviticus 18.12.) Aaron married Elisheba, the sister of Nahshon. Nahshon became the leader of the people of Judah, Numbers 2.3. Aaron's sons were called Nadab, Abihu, Eleazar and Ithamar. The name of Eleazar's son was Phinehas. We will read of all these men later on. This is the family of Aaron and Moses, the men whom God sent to Pharaoh, vs.26,27.

Still they were afraid to go. Jehovah told them that Moses would be as God to Pharaoh and Aaron would be Moses' prophet. They must tell Pharaoh what God had said. Still Pharaoh would close his heart. He would not let Israel go before God showed many great wonders. After this Moses and Aaron were willing to go to Pharaoh. Moses was 80 years old by now and his brother Aaron 83, 7.1-7.

If you are ever afraid to tell anyone about your Saviour, remember Moses and Aaron. These men were afraid to go in to Pharaoh, but when they went great things began to happen. When God called Jeremiah, the young man did not think he was able to serve as a prophet of God. The Lord gave him enough strength, Jeremiah 1.4-10.

The first signs, 7.8-13.

God had given Moses three signs for the children of Israel, 4.1-9. These signs convinced the people of Israel that the LORD had really sent Moses and Aaron, 4.29-31. Now the Lord told Moses

17

and Aaron to show the first sign to Pharaoh, vs.8-13. Aaron threw down the rod before Pharaoh and it became a snake. Pharaoh called his own priests and they were able to do the same thing. However Aaron's rod ate up the rods of the Egyptians. God sometimes lets the servants of Satan do great signs, Matthew 24.24, Revelation 13.13, but God is always in control and over all. Pharaoh closed his heart and he would not believe that God had sent Moses and Aaron.

We should not believe false teachers even though they can do wonderful things. Do not accept any man unless he teaches the truth and gives glory to the Lord Jesus Christ.

The first plague: The river became blood, 7.14-25.

God had promised Moses that Pharaoh would let Israel go, but first He had to deal ten heavy blows on Egypt. The history of these ten plagues is in chapters 7 to 12. God had given Moses three signs, 4.1-9, and now God used the third sign as the first plague on Egypt. Moses and Aaron met Pharaoh on the way to the river. This river, the great river Nile, runs through desert land. Without the river people could not live in Egypt. The people grow their food only by using the water of the river. Moses spoke to Pharaoh in the name of the God of the Hebrews and warned him to let the people go. Moses told Pharaoh that he would turn the water of the river into blood. The fish would die and the people would have nothing to drink.

Pharaoh did not pay any attention to this warning, so Aaron held up the rod over the Nile river and the water turned to blood. Even the water in pots turned to blood and the people had nothing to drink. However the priests of Egypt were able to do the same, and Pharaoh's heart was hardened.

The second plague: Frogs, 8.1-15.

After seven days Moses went again to Pharaoh and told him that the Lord wanted His people to go. If Pharaoh refused, God would bring a plague of *frogs* on the land. These little creatures live in and near the water. They cannot hurt a man but many thousands of them jumping all over the place would be very unpleasant. Pharaoh did not pay any attention to Moses' warning, so Aaron raised his rod and the frogs came up all over the land. The priests of Egypt were able to bring up frogs by their secret tricks.

This time however Pharaoh called for Moses and Aaron. He told them to ask the Lord to take away the frogs. If He did, Pharaoh would let Israel go. The next day Moses prayed to Jehovah and the frogs died. The people gathered the dead frogs together into smelly heaps. However Pharaoh saw that the frogs were gone and he hardened his heart, just as the Lord had said.

The third plague: Gnats, 8.16-19.

Moses did not give any warning for the third plague. Aaron just lifted up his rod and the dust of the land of Egypt turned into gnats or fleas, little flying creatures that bite. The priests of Egypt tried to do this also, but could not. They agreed that God was helping Israel, but still Pharaoh's heart was hard and he would not listen to Moses.

The fourth plague: Flies, 8.20-32.

This time Moses warned Pharaoh what the Lord would do. If Pharaoh would not let Israel go, God would send flies to the land of Egypt. He would not send them to the land of Goshen where the people of Israel were. These flies were so bad that Pharaoh called Moses and Aaron and made a half-way suggestion. Pharaoh told Moses and Aaron that Israel could sacrifice to their God *in the land of Egypt,* v.25. Moses refused this plan. The people of Egypt worshipped many gods including the holy cow. If Israel killed a cow the Egyptians would make trouble for them. They might try to kill the Israelites with stones. Moses demanded that they go three days' journey into the wilderness. Pharaoh made another half-way suggestion. Israel could go a *little* distance into the wilderness. Moses agreed to pray that the Lord would take away the flies. At the same time he warned Pharaoh not to change his mind again, v.29. When the flies were gone, Pharaoh again hardened his heart.

At first Moses had been afraid to go in to Pharaoh. By now his faith in Jehovah was greater. Moses is now confident enough to talk firmly to Pharaoh. We are all the same. At first we may be afraid of doing something hard, but the Lord gives strength if we just try.

Note also that the word *division* in verse 23 means *redemption.* The Lord is always willing to make a difference between His children and the people of the world. God will redeem any sinner who wants to escape God's judgment on the world. The sinner should put his trust in Christ. If he refuses to believe he must take the results and suffer with the world.

The fifth plague: Disease of animals, 9.1-7.

Moses again brought the message of the Lord to Pharaoh: *"Let my people go that they may serve me."* He warned Pharaoh that Jehovah would send a disease on the animals of Egypt. Again the Lord made a difference between the animals of Israel and the animals of Egypt. Pharaoh saw that the cattle of the Israelites were still alive and his heart was hardened. He simply took some of Israel's cattle for himself. In the next plague judgment fell again on the cattle of Egypt, v.9.

The sixth plague: Sores, 9.8-12.

Moses gave Pharaoh no warning of the sixth plague. At the command of Jehovah Moses and Aaron simply took ashes of burnt wood in their hands and threw them up in the air. The ashes became dust and made sores come out on the skin of men and animals. These sores came on the priests as well. They too were under the judgment of God.

Although God had proved His power in many ways, we have seen that Pharaoh hardened his heart, 8.15,32. We read also that the **Lord** hardened Pharaoh's heart, 9.12; 10.1,20,27 and 11.10. Both of these things were true. Pharaoh refused to yield to God and obey Him. He *"hardened his heart."* God had promised that He would deliver His people, so He kept on giving Pharaoh more and more proof of His own power. He *"hardened Pharaoh's heart."*

This does not mean that Pharaoh as a man had no way to be saved. God is righteous and gives every person a way to be saved. In Pharaoh's case he saw many signs of God's power, yet kept on hardening his heart. At last he brought destruction on himself and on his nation. Read Romans 9.17.

The seventh plague: Hail, 9.13-35.

The Lord again commanded Moses to stand before Pharaoh. He should plainly warn him of the results of his foolish acts. Pharaoh had done wrong in making the people of Israel work for nothing. He did worse by commanding that all baby boys should be killed. He kept on refusing to let Israel go and so must take his punishment. God allowed him to live a little longer so that He could show all men His power, v.16, Romans 9.17. Moses told Pharaoh and the people of Egypt that there would be a terrible storm the next day. Some of the Egyptians believed the word of Moses and brought their slaves and animals into their houses, v.20.

The next day Moses lifted his rod and the Lord sent the hail. These hard little stones can often fall from the clouds in such great numbers that they will destroy the crops. Sometimes they are so large that they will destroy men and animals. This is what happened that day. The hail destroyed trees and plants, animals and men in all Egypt. The hail did not fall in the land of Goshen.

This time Pharaoh seemed to be really sorry, vs.27-33. Moses agreed to pray to the Lord, but he knew that Pharaoh had not really repented. Some of the crops were still so small that the hail had not destroyed them. Again Pharaoh and his men hardened their hearts against Jehovah, vs.34,35.

This should warn us not to repent and then go back to our sins again. God may stop punishing us for a short time, but if we sin again, He will punish us still more.

The eighth plague: Locusts, 10.1-20.

This time Moses and Aaron went to Pharaoh and told him that the Lord would send locusts. These small creatures flying in very great numbers can quickly eat up the grain and grass of a whole country. Moses and Aaron told Pharaoh to be more humble and obey the Lord. If he still refused, the Lord would send so many locusts into Egypt that a person would not be able to see the ground. These locusts would eat every leaf and every bit of grass that was left after the storm, Psalm 105.34,35. The locusts would also fill the houses of the people.

Some of Pharaoh's servants believed this warning and they told Pharaoh to let Israel go, vs.7-11. Pharaoh called Moses and Aaron and told them to go and serve the Lord. Then he quickly asked who would go. Moses said that they all would go and all their animals as well. Pharaoh became very angry and said he would let only the men go. He knew that this plan would make the men return to Egypt for their families. Pharaoh at once sent Moses and Aaron away from him, v.11.

Moses lifted up his rod over the land of Egypt. The Lord brought an east wind and the next day the locusts came by the thousands. They covered the earth and ate every leaf and every bit of grass left in the land. Pharaoh called for Moses and Aaron to come back to him. Again he said that he had sinned, 9.27. He asked Moses to forgive his sin, v.17. Then the Lord sent a strong west wind which drove the locusts into the Red Sea. Again Pharaoh's heart was hardened, v.20.

The ninth plague: Darkness, 10.21-29.

For the third, sixth and ninth plague Pharaoh received no warning ahead of time. In the first three plagues Aaron used the rod and in the seventh and eighth plague Moses used it. The rod is not mentioned for plagues 4, 5 and 6, and in the ninth Moses just lifted up his hand toward heaven. When he did Jehovah sent thick darkness over all Egypt for three days. In many ways this was the most terrible of all the plagues. The Lord had kept the flies and the hail from the land of Goshen. In the time of the ninth plague also the people of Israel had light in their houses. This time Pharaoh was again willing to let the people go, but he told them to leave their *animals* in Egypt. Again Moses refused and said that all the animals must go as well. So the Lord hardened Pharaoh's heart still more, v.28. Pharaoh became so angry that he told Moses to go and never come to see him again. If he did he would die.

From all this we must learn the terrible results of rejecting God and refusing to believe in Him. God sent His Son to die on the cross for our sins and to rise again from the dead. This is a far greater sign than any shown to Pharaoh. God often speaks to men today by sending them trouble of different kinds, Job 33.14-30. Sometimes even believers refuse the leading of the Lord and will not obey His commands. They are sure to suffer for this. God does not want anyone to perish, 2 Peter 3.9, 1 Timothy 2.4, but there is no salvation for those who keep on refusing.

In the book of Revelation we read of a time of great trouble yet to come to this world. There we read of locusts, Revelation 9.3,7; darkness, 16.10; frogs, 16.13; and hail, 16 21. However these things are probably *pictures* of the terrible trouble which is yet to come.

Lesson 3
THE PASSOVER AND THE EXODUS, chapters 11,12.

God sent Moses to lead His people out of Egypt, but Pharaoh refused to let Israel go. God sent nine judgments, one after another, on Pharaoh and on Egypt. The tenth plague was the death of every first-born son in all Egypt. After this Pharaoh **commanded** Israel to get out of his country.

Chapter 11 follows on from chapter 10 without a break. After the ninth plague (darkness) Pharaoh tried to tell Moses that they should leave their animals in Egypt. When Moses refused Pharaoh became very angry. If Moses ever came to see him again Pharaoh would kill him. While he was still standing before Pharaoh, Moses remembered what Jehovah had said to him before. Only one more plague would be necessary, 11.1. The people of Israel should ask their neighbours to give them silver and gold. The people of Israel had worked for many years without any pay. This silver and gold would be only a part of the money which they had earned. The Egyptians and Pharaoh's servants were afraid of Moses and they honoured the people of Israel, v.3.

Then Moses told Pharaoh what would happen, vs.4-8. About the middle of the night Jehovah would go through the land of Egypt and the oldest son in every family would die. Even Pharaoh's oldest son would not be saved. No one would say or do anything against the people of Israel. The men of Egypt would bow down to Moses and ask him to leave their country. Moses was still very angry; when he had said these things he went out from Pharaoh. Still the Lord told Moses that Pharaoh would not hear him, vs.9,10.

The Passover, 12.1-20.

In the first 20 verses of chapter 12 the Lord gave commands about the first Passover and the feast which the people of Israel were to keep every year. Moses passed these commands on to the people, vs.21-27. The rest of this chapter tells us how Israel left the land of Egypt.

When the Lord led Israel out of Egypt, He destroyed the oldest child in every family. Jehovah passed over every house where blood had been put on the outside. So the Lord commanded Israel to remember every year this great deliverance feast, which is called the Passover. It was so important that Israel called that month the **first** month of the year, v.2. The name of the first month was Abib, 34.18. On the tenth day of that month the head of every house

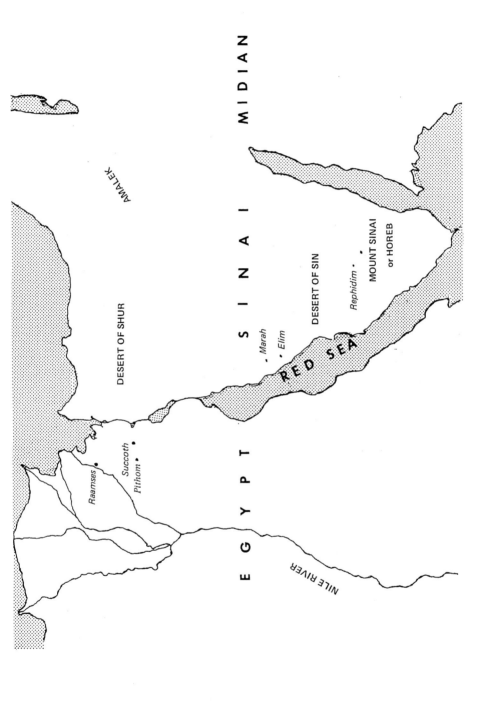

was to take a lamb or a young goat for his family. If the family was small, two neighbours would go together on one animal. It had to be a male, one year old. The most important thing was this: they could not use an animal that was blind or had anything wrong with it. It had to be perfect, v.5.

The lamb was to be watched for four days and on the fourteenth day it was killed in the evening. The blood was put outside the house on the doorposts. The meat was cooked on the fire and eaten with bread and bitter greens. They could not eat the meat if it was not cooked or if it was boiled with water. They had to eat all the meat and if any was left over, they should burn it in the fire. While they were eating the meat they had to be all ready to leave on their journey, v.11.

Jehovah was going to kill the oldest child in every home and also the first-born of every animal, vs.12,13. He would also bring judgment against the false gods of Egypt. He promised to pass over any house on which the blood had been placed on the outside.

Any of the Egyptians could have been saved in this way if they had believed the word of the Lord. We do not read that any Egyptians did so, but there may have been some. A mixed group of people left Egypt with Israel, v.38. Some of these may have been Egyptians. Strangers who wished to live with Israel could keep the feast of the Passover, 12.48. The grace of God is great enough to save anyone who believes.

The passover lamb speaks of our Lord Jesus Christ, the perfect Lamb of God. As sinners we were in the power of Satan and under the judgment of God, but a perfect Lamb has laid down His life. The blood on the door posts outside the house told all men that the lamb had been slain. All who were in the house were safe. This message to men outside is important. To be saved we are told to confess with our lips that Jesus is Lord as well as believe in our hearts, Romans 10.9. Unless men know that we belong to Christ, they will expect us to go on in sin. God wants to save us from sin every day.

If the family was too small for a whole lamb the man should call in his neighbour's family to join with them. We know that Christ is more than enough for us. We should share Him with others. Our Lord Jesus Christ is a great Saviour, great enough for the whole world. He commanded us to offer His salvation to neighbours, friends and relations.

Inside the house, saved by the blood, the people were feasting on

25

the lamb. We who are saved should read the Word of God. As we think about the Lord Jesus Christ we will get pleasure and strength for the journey. The fire speaks of the judgment of God which our Lord Jesus took for us. Killing the lamb and cooking the meat both make us think of Christ's death. When the Lord Jesus was alive He could not save us from sin. In His death it was necessary that He should bear the full judgment of God. The fire speaks of God's judgment.

When a baker mixes up the flour to make bread he puts in yeast or leaven to make it rise. Just a little yeast soon spreads through all the flour. In the same way sin spreads among the people. In the Bible yeast is a picture of spreading evil, 1 Corinthians 5.6-8. Bread made without yeast speaks of the purity of our Lord Jesus Christ. There was no sin in Him, 1 Peter 2.22. With the lamb the Israelites ate bread made without yeast. They also ate bitter greens which may speak of sorrows in the life of our Lord Jesus, Isaiah 53.3. Every day we can enjoy precious thoughts of Christ's purity, His sorrows and death.

Jehovah told Moses that they should keep the feast of unleavened bread every year, vs.14-20. This feast lasted for one week following the Passover. From the fourteenth day of the first month to the twenty first day they could not eat any bread with yeast in it. Anyone who did so would be put out of the nation of Israel, vs.15,19. Later in the Law Moses told Israel to keep the feasts of the Lord. The command about the Passover and the feast of unleavened bread is found in Leviticus 23.4-8.

Moses gave these commands to the people, 12.21-27.

When Moses had received these commands from Jehovah he called together the leaders of Israel. He told them to kill the Passover lamb and to catch the blood in a pot. Then they should take a little hyssop or grass and put the blood on the upper door post and two side posts. Everybody had to stay inside the house until the morning.

The feast of the Passover was to be kept every year for ever. The fathers should explain to their children what the Passover meant. When Jehovah destroyed the Egyptians He *passed over* the houses of Israel.

The Exodus, 12.28-51.

As Jehovah had said, all the first-born children died in the middle of the night. The first-born of great men and the first-born of the common people, all died. The first-born of animals died also. Pharaoh himself rose up in the night and a great cry went up from Egypt. The oldest child in every house was dead! Pharaoh called for Moses and Aaron and commanded them to go, and take all their animals with them. He even asked Moses and Aaron to bless him! Moses had said that he would not see Pharaoh again, 10.29, so it seems that Pharaoh sent this message to him by his servants. The Egyptians were afraid that they would all be killed. They wanted to see the Israelites go away as quickly as possible. The Egyptians gave them silver and gold and clothing. This was a very small return for all the work which the Israelites had done in Egypt without pay. The Israelites left in such a hurry that they did not have time to prepare their bread. They just took it the way it was before they put in the yeast, v.34.

The first part of the journey was from Rameses to Succoth, v.37. There were about 600,000 men besides the women and children. About a year later Moses numbered the men of Israel who were old enough to go to war. At that time the number was 603,550, Numbers 1.46. With all the women and children there must have been about 3 million people who left Egypt. In addition there was a mixed group, v.38.

All the time the people lived in Egypt was 430 years, v.40. This may mean it was 430 years from the time Abraham first went to Egypt, Galatians 3.17. The Exodus was so important that the Lord commanded Israel to remember it forever, v.42.

What about the strangers who lived with the people of Israel? The Lord gave Moses commands about them, vs.43-49. If a man bought a servant, the servant could be circumcised and join in the feast of the Passover. A foreigner or a visitor could not eat with the people of Israel. A servant who was paid money could not share in the Passover feast. If a foreigner wanted to be circumcised he could then join with the people of God in this service.

The people of Israel kept the feast of the Passover one year later, Numbers 9.1,2. They also kept the feast in the time of:

Joshua, Joshua 5.10
Hezekiah, 2 Chronicles 30.1
Josia, 2 Chronicles 35.1
Zerrubbabel, Ezra 6.19

These are the only verses in the Old Testament about the Passover. Through all the history of Israel those who were faithful to the Lord no doubt kept the Passover year after year, 2 Chronicles

8.13. When Israel did not walk with the Lord they did not obey this commandment, 2 Chronicles 30.5.

In New Testament times those who were faithful in Israel went up every year to Jerusalem for the feast of the Passover, Luke 2.41. While the Lord Jesus was on earth we read of three other feasts of the Passover, John 2.23; 6.4; 13.1.

Christ our Passover Lamb has been sacrificed, 1 Corinthians 5.7. The Passover of Old Testament days looked forward to the death of Christ. We Christians look **back** to the death of Christ. We should break the bread and remember Him each Lord's Day, 1 Corinthians 11.24, Acts 20.7.

The Exodus marks the beginning of the history of Israel. Many times they looked back to the great day when the Lord brought them out of Egypt. Moses told them that this should make them want to trust the Lord, Deuteronomy 1.30; 29.2. Joshua told them again about that great day, Joshua 24.6. So did a prophet of the Lord, Judges 6.8; so did Samuel, 1 Samuel 10.18, and Jeremiah, Jeremiah 2.6. The story is told again in Psalm 78.43-51 and 105. 23-38. In the New Testament we read that through **faith** Moses kept the Passover, Hebrews 11.28.

When Israel was delivered from Egypt, it was the beginning of a new year, 12.2. When a sinner is delivered from the power of Satan, it is the beginning of a new **life** for him, 2 Corinthians 5.17. The Holy Spirit inspired the writers of the Old Testament and now lives within the believer. The Spirit is always trying to help us think about the Lord Jesus Christ. So in the story of the Passover lamb we can see many beautiful pictures of Christ. As we think about Him we will become more like Him.

Lesson 4

THE JOURNEY THROUGH THE WILDERNESS, chapters 13-18.

We now come to the second of the three main parts of the book of Exodus. In chapter 1 we saw Israel in the land of Egypt. At the end of the book they are at Mount Sinai.

Exodus 1-12   Israel in Egypt
Exodus 13-18   Israel travelled from Egypt to Mount Sinai.
Exodus 19-40   Israel at Mount Sinai

Instructions to the people, 13.1-16.

God had said that all the first-born children in Egypt were His. They were saved from death if blood was put on the door posts. Even so all the first-born belonged to God, both man and animal, vs.1,2.

Joseph and Mary, the mother of the Lord Jesus, knew this command. When Jesus was born Joseph and Mary brought their offering to Jehovah, Luke 2.23,24. As Christians we must remember that **all** our children belong to the Lord. We are told to bring them up for God, Ephesians 6.4.

After receiving this command Moses spoke to the people of Israel. First he told them again of the feast of unleavened bread. They should keep this feast in the month Abib, while in the wilderness and when they reached the land of promise, vs.3-10. Each father should teach his son the reason for keeping the feast, v.8.

Then Moses commanded the people about the first-born, vs.11-16. He told them that the first **male** born into any family belonged to God. This meant that an offering must be brought to the Lord instead of the child. The first-born male of a clean animal must be sacrificed to the Lord. A clean animal had to be sacrificed instead of the first-born male of an unclean animal. We will see the difference between clean and unclean animals in Leviticus 11.

Note that only the **unclean** animal could live, and then only if another animal died for it. Here is a picture of the sinner. All men **are** sinful and unclean, but many will not accept this fact. If they do, it is simple to point them to the Lamb of God who died for them, Luke 5.32. If there was no sacrifice for the unclean animal, it had to die also, v.13.

Moses told the people to remember these commands and pass them on to their children. These commands should be like a sign on the hand or between the eyes, vs.9,16. This means that the

Israelites were always to remember these things.

Crossing the Red Sea, 13.17 - 14.31.

The rest of the chapter, vs.17-22, tells us about the first part of Israel's travels. The most direct way from Egypt to the land of Canaan lies through the country of the Philistines. God saw that it was best to lead the people by a longer way. When they became a strong nation they would be ready to fight against their enemies. God knew that Israel had many lessons to learn. This longer way took them to the Red Sea.

Before leaving Egypt Moses remembered that Joseph had asked them to bury his bones in the land of Canaan, Genesis 50.25. When Israel left Egypt, the people took Joseph's bones with them. Through the long desert the people would often remember their saviour of earlier years.

The apostle Paul always remembered the death of the Lord Jesus Christ, 2 Corinthians 4.10. As we walk through this world we should always remember that we have been crucified with Christ, Galatians 2.20.

The Lord led Israel through the wilderness by a cloud in the day time. This also kept them from the hot sun, Psalm 105.39. At night the fire gave them light. All through the desert journey they knew that God was with them. The Lord Jesus has promised to be with us to keep and to guide us, Matthew 28.20. Why should we be afraid?

The Lord led Israel through the desert toward the Red Sea. Pharaoh saw that he might yet be able to bring Israel back as slaves. The Lord told Moses that He would harden Pharaoh's heart and Pharaoh would follow Israel, 14.1-4. God had warned Pharaoh many times and now He is ready to judge him.

Pharaoh told his men that letting Israel go was a foolish thing. Pharaoh and the army of the Egyptians started out with all their chariots after Israel. Horses can pull chariots very quickly and the Egyptians soon caught up to the people of Israel, vs.5-9. Each chariot would hold at least one soldier with sword and spear. No wonder the people of Israel were afraid of them!

In fact they were in great fear, vs.10-18. In that minute they lost all their faith in God. They asked Moses why he had not let them stay in Egypt. Live slaves of Pharaoh would be better than dead men in the wilderness. Moses' faith however was as strong as ever. He knew that the Lord would work for them that day. They would never see the Egyptians again, v.13. Jehovah told Moses that this was not the time to pray but to act. The people of Israel should move forward toward the sea. Moses should lift up his rod and the people would go through on dry ground. The Egyptians would try to follow, but the Lord would get the victory.

Have you ever been in a difficulty like this? The people of Israel did not know which way to move. Mountains were on both sides and the Egyptians behind them and the sea in front of them. They were afraid that they would all be killed. Moses commanded the people to stand still and not run away. Then God told them to go forward. When we do not know which way to turn, we should quietly wait on the Lord until He shows us what to do.

First the Angel of God and the cloud moved from before Israel to a place behind them, vs.19,20. For this reason the Egyptians could not attack Israel that night, vs.19,20.

The Lord also sent a strong east wind which made a dry path through the sea. The Israelites started to cross over. They walked on dry ground and the waters were like a wall on both sides of them. You would think that this great miracle would now at last convince the Egyptians. Surely they would know that God was with Israel. Instead of that they followed them into the sea. The Lord let the Egyptians go so far. The morning watch is the last three hours of the night just before day. When their chariot wheels would not turn smoothly, the Egyptians saw they were in trouble. Then they knew that the Lord was fighting for Israel, but it was too late, vs.21-25.

Moses lifted up his hand over the sea and the waters came back to their usual place. All Pharaoh's men and their horses died in the sea. This was in the same place where the people of Israel had walked through on dry ground. For Israel the water was like a wall on both sides, vs.26-29.

The men of Israel saw the dead bodies of the Egyptians on the land at the edge of the sea. The people feared the Lord and knew that He had sent Moses to be their leader, vs.30,31.

The sinner today needs to be saved by blood and by power. By the blood of Christ God is able to forgive our sins and deliver us from the judgment of the Law. The Passover lamb speaks of this. All the first-born in the land of Goshen were under the judgment of death. Only the blood of a perfect lamb saved them.

God does more than forgive my sins. He delivers me from the **power** of sin. When I first trusted in Christ I had many bad and

31

sinful habits. These had ruled in my life for many years. God forgave my sins that day, but in myself I did not have the strength to overcome these bad habits. When I accepted Christ as Saviour, God gave me also the gift of the Holy Spirit. He gives me power to overcome temptation. When Israel passed through the Red Sea, God delivered them from the power of Pharaoh. The Red Sea is a picture of God's power in the believer to help him overcome sinful habits.

The song of Israel, chapter 15.

Moses and the people of Israel sang a song of victory and thanksgiving to the Lord. This is the first song of praise in the Bible. Moses also wrote Psalm 90. Later on the saints will sing the song of Moses, the servant of God, and the song of the Lamb, Revelation 15.3.

What is this song in Exodus 15 about? Moses sang to Jehovah because of His great victory, vs.1-3. Jehovah was the God of Moses and of his father. Like a man of war the Lord fought for His people. Moses led the people of Israel in singing this song of victory.

In this song Moses told the story of the Lord's victory, vs.4-12. God had thrown the armies of Pharaoh into the Red Sea, vs.4,5. This showed God's great power, vs.6,7. By the east wind He made the waters stand in a heap, v.8. The enemies of Israel wanted to get their money or to kill them, v.9. God just sent His wind and the Egyptians sank in the water as heavy metal would sink, v.10. Moses knew that Jehovah was greater than all the gods, v.11.

Looking ahead to the future Moses saw that other nations would soon hear about this great victory. God was going to lead His people Israel to the land of Canaan. Philistia is part of Canaan and the countries of Edom and Moab are close by. All these people would be very much afraid when they heard what Jehovah had done. Moses was sure that the Lord would bring Israel into their own land. Jehovah would reign for ever and ever, vs.13-18.

Verse 19 tells again the reason for the song. Miriam, the sister of Moses and Aaron, led the women in their praise to God, vs.20, 21.

When Israel crossed over the Red Sea on dry ground, they praised the Lord, but their troubles were not over. Moses led them into the desert and they could not find any water to drink. At last they did find some water at a place called Marah, but it was too bitter to drink. They spoke against Moses and Moses prayed to the Lord. The Lord showed him a certain tree which made the water sweet.

Even when God is leading us we will have trials and problems. God plans these to make our faith stronger and to make us more like the Lord Jesus. God works all things together for good that we might become more like His Son, Romans 8.28,29. Israel in the desert is a picture of the believer in this world. God has not promised that the Christian life would be pure joy and happiness. In fact the Lord Jesus told us that we will have trouble in this world, John 16.33. The Holy Spirit also warns us of sufferings, 1 Thessalonians 3.3, Philippians 1.29.

At Marah the Lord was testing Israel, vs. 23-26. He also promised them a blessing if they would obey His commands. He would keep them from the diseases which were common in Egypt. He said, *"I am Jehovah your Healer."* God made the water sweet. He could also heal His people.

In the New Testament the Lord Jesus and His followers healed many sick people. This proved that God had sent them into the world with His message. God is still able to answer prayer and thousands of Christians can tell how the Lord healed them. There is no promise however that we will never be sick. In fact some of the greatest saints are sick most of the time.

At Marah the Lord tested His people and soon found out what was in their hearts. If they had believed in God they would not have grumbled to Moses. They spoke to Moses, but they were really blaming God. This was a terrible sin. The tree cut down makes us think of the Lord Jesus Christ who died for us. As we remember His sufferings on the cross we can face the problems of life without grumbling. His cross makes the bitter waters sweet.

At last they came to Elim where there was plenty of water and also some fruit trees, v.27. So they rested there for a few days. The Lord will never give us too much trial or temptation. He sends the sunshine and the rain, good days and hard days. When we are tempted He always gives a way of escape, 1 Corinthians 10.13.

The Manna, chapter 16.

A month after Israel had left Egypt, they reached the desert of Sin between Elim and Mount Sinai. The people of Israel fell into sin again, but this is not the reason for calling the place the desert of Sin. Through the whole journey to the Promised Land the people of Israel very often fell into sin. Here they grumbled for the third time, vs.1-3; 14.11; 15.24. This time they grumbled because they had no food. Again they looked back to earlier days in

Egypt, where they at least got enough to eat. They said that Moses had brought them out into the desert to kill them.

The people really needed food, but their words show they did not trust God at all. To meet their need the Lord promised Moses that He would give Israel bread from heaven, vs.4-8. This was also a test to see if the people would walk in God's law and rest on the seventh day. In the beginning God had set aside the seventh day as a day of rest, Genesis 2.3. While in Egypt no doubt Israel could not rest on the seventh day or any other day. Now God told Israel that on the sixth day of every week they could gather enough food for two days. No bread would be given on the seventh day, but they would have enough to eat. So Israel's need for food and God's supply formed another test of Israel's love and obedience.

Moses and Aaron told the children of Israel that in the evening and the morning God would glorify Himself, vs.6,7. The people of Israel were not speaking against Moses and Aaron, but against Jehovah, v.8. Moses said that in the evening God would give them meat to eat and in the morning bread.

The Lord Jesus called Himself the **Bread of Life**. His flesh is food indeed, John 6.35,55. Though we are saved by blood and by the power of God, we need to feed on Christ every day of our journey through this world. God supplies all our needs in Christ.

Moses told Aaron to gather the whole company together to hear what God would say, vs.9-12. Suddenly all the people saw the glory of the Lord in the cloud. The Lord said that He had heard the grumbling of Israel. He would give them meat to eat in the evening and bread every morning.

The Lord gave them food as He had promised, but some of the people did not obey His command, vs.13-21. That very evening a great number of birds came up and covered the camp. In the morning the people saw a small round thing on the ground. They did not know what it was, but Moses told them it was bread for them to eat. Some of the people gathered a lot of the bread, but they could not eat it all. God gave the birds only once at this time, but He gave them bread every morning. Later Israel grumbled again and God gave the birds again for a whole month, Numbers 11.18-20, 31.

On the sixth day they gathered enough food for two days. Moses told them to cook it and it would be good to eat on the seventh day. The leaders came to Moses to be sure that everything was alright, vs.22-30. The people had enough food left over from the sixth day, but still some went out on the seventh day. No wonder the Lord became angry with them. Again He commanded them to rest on the seventh day. In this chapter for the first time in the Bible we see the seventh day is called the sabbath, vs.23,25,26,29. We will read more about the sabbath in 20.8-11.

The people called the bread *manna.* It was white and tasted sweet, vs.31-36. The Lord commanded Moses to take a pot made of gold and fill it with the manna. This would help the children of Israel to remember how the Lord fed them in the desert. This gold pot was later put into a box with the tables of stone and with Aaron's rod, Hebrews 9.4. The people ate manna for forty years, but when they got to the land of promise, God did not give them any more manna, Joshua 5.12. In Psalm 78 we have an account of God's dealings with Israel. Manna is called angels' food, Psalm 78.25. Also read Psalm 78.12-14; 105.26-41; 106.7-15.

In this chapter we see God's loving supply for the needs of His people. We also see that they grumbled against God and some of them did not obey His commands. May the Lord teach us to love and obey Him without grumbling!

Water from the rock, 17.1-7.

The Lord commanded Israel to move forward and they came to Rephidim. This is near Mount Horeb or Mount Sinai. The people were still getting manna every morning, but now there was no water to drink. So the people spoke against Moses again. This was the fourth time. Moses asked, "Why do you blame me?" Why did they have to ask if God was really caring for them? The thirsty people accused Moses of bringing them up from Egypt to kill them with thirst. Moses saw that they were ready to kill him and he cried to the Lord. The Lord told him to take the rod of God in his hand and to go out with the elders of the people. Jehovah stood on the rock at Horeb. Moses struck the rock with the rod and the water came pouring out. God looked after the needs of His people by giving them water. Moses called the place Massah and Meribah because the people grumbled there.

This rock speaks of Christ as the Son of God. Just as a great rock is solid and does not seem to change, so the Son of God is eternal and unchanging, John 1.1, Hebrews 1.8. The word rock is a name of God, Deuteronomy 32.4,15,18,30,31. Peter said to the Lord, *"You are the Christ, the Son of the living God."* The Lord answered him and said, *"On this rock I will build my church,"*

Matthew 16.16-18. The Lord Jesus did not mean that He would build His church on poor failing Peter. He would build His church on the great truth that He Himself is God. In Exodus 17 when Moses struck the rock, the water of life came out. Moses here is a picture of the Law of God. According to the Law of God we sinners have to die for our sins. The Lord Jesus Christ paid the price for us. He met the demands of the Law and now gives life to all, John 4.10,14; 7.37.

In this story again we see the Lord leading His people into difficult places, then showing His power to them. In the same way the Lord Jesus went to the desert and 5000 people followed Him. When they had no food He wonderfully supplied all, John 6.5-13. In another place when He knew that Lazarus was sick He did not go and cure him, but waited until His friend had died. In raising Lazarus from the dead the Lord got much more glory than by healing him from sickness, John 11.6,43-45. We should learn to trust Him in time of trouble without grumbling. We can be sure He will help at the right time.

The struggle with Amalek, 17.8-16.

This world is like a desert for us, but God gives everything we need through our Lord Jesus Christ. He also gives victory in the struggle with our enemy. While Israel was still in Rephidim the people of Amalek came out to fight with them. Moses called a young man, Joshua, and said, *"Choose some good men and go out to fight with Amalek."* Joshua later became a brave man who really believed God. When Moses died Joshua became the leader of Israel. Joshua's first lesson was this: **Only prayer can win battles for the Lord.** Three men, Moses, Aaron and Hur, went to the top of the hill. Hur belonged to the tribe of Judah. In later years his son's son, Bezalel, became the leader in building the tabernacle, 31.1-11.

When Moses held up his hands in prayer the army of Israel started to win in the battle. When Moses was tired, he let his hands down and Amalek started to win. So Aaron and Hur held up his hands until the victory was won.

Today in the spiritual battle with our enemy only prayer can give the victory. Happily we have a great High Priest who never gets tired of praying for us, Hebrews 7.25. We too should keep on praying for the Lord's servants so the enemy will not get the victory over them. Paul often asked the believers to pray for him, 2 Corinthians 1.11, Ephesians 6.18,19, Colossians 4.3, 1 Thessalonians 5.25, 2 Thessalonians 3.1.

The Lord commanded Moses to write the story of this victory in a book and to teach Joshua these lessons, vs.14-16. Moses was writing this history of the Lord's dealings with Israel which we now call the book of Exodus. The Lord said He would make all people forget about Amalek. However the struggle would continue for a long time.

Amalek was the son of Esau's son, Genesis 36.10,12. Esau was not a spiritual man, Hebrews 12.16, and Amalek speaks of the **flesh** as an enemy of the true believer. As long as a believer is alive he has the old nature in him. There is always a struggle between the flesh and the Spirit, Galatians 5.16-24. Only when the Lord comes will we lose this old nature. Then we will be changed and be like Him, 1 John 3.2. Every day we can gain the victory over the flesh by walking in the Spirit, Galatians 5.16; by putting on the Lord Jesus Christ, Romans 13.14, and by seeing ourselves as dead unto sin, Romans 6.11, and crucified with Christ, Galatians 2.20. Read these verses carefully.

After this great victory Moses built an altar and called it *"The Lord is my banner."* A banner or flag is used in a war. When men see the flag they want to fight for their country. God's banner over us is love, Song of Solomon 2.4. When we remember the love of God to us we want to love Him as well. This will give us strength for the great struggle of life and the Lord will give us the victory.

Jethro the priest of Midian, chapter 18.

Jethro the father of Moses' wife was also called Reuel, Exodus 2.18, Numbers 10.29. It seems that Moses' wife had left him after he circumcised their son and returned to her father, 4.25,26. After many months Jethro brought Zipporah and the two sons back to Moses, vs.1-9. Moses had named his sons according to the problems and blessings of his own life. Moses lived as a stranger in the land of Midian and he called his first son Gershom which means *"a stranger there."* It also was the name of the oldest son of Levi, 1 Chronicles 6.16. Moses was a stranger in the land of Midian but the Lord blessed him there. He called his other son Eliezer which means *"my God is a help."* This was also the name of Abraham's servant, Genesis 15.2.

When his wife's father arrived Moses welcomed him and they talked together in Moses' tent. Moses told Jethro all that the Lord had done for Israel. Jethro agreed that Jehovah was greater than all gods. This does not mean that he turned to Jehovah and believed in Him. At.the end of the chapter he left the people of God and went back to his own land. Jethro even offered a burnt offering and sacrifices to God, v.12, but these things do not prove that he had really put his trust in the one true God.

Many people say that they "believe" in God and even that they "believe" in Christ. This is not the same as trusting the Lord as your own Saviour, John 2.23,24.

The next day Moses sat with the people and listened to all their troubles. If there was a quarrel between two people, Moses listened to both sides and told them what was right. Jethro was wise in the things of this world and thought that all this work would make Moses too tired. Jethro suggested that he should set up a system of judges. They would be able to judge all small matters. If a problem was too hard for them, they could bring it to Moses, vs.13-23.

Moses did as his wife's father had suggested, but there is no sign that he first asked the Lord about it. Jehovah had supplied enough strength for Moses up to this time. If Moses needed more help he could have asked God about it. It was Moses' duty to make the people know the laws of God, v.16. Moses gave authority to these men, over 60,000 of them. No doubt many of them were good men and this step may seem like a good thing to do.

Sometimes people of this world may tell us to do a good thing, but we should always ask the Lord to guide us. We all need wisdom to do the right thing in this world. God will freely give us wisdom and will not blame us for asking for it, James 1.5.

Lesson 5
THE LAW OF MOSES, chapters 19-24.

When God gave the Law at Mount Sinai it was one of the greatest events in history. In six chapters, 19-24, we have the facts of what took place at that time. In other parts of the Bible we learn the meaning of the Law. This is the first and only time when God gave His Law to His people. In chapter 19 Moses prepared the people for this great event. Then God called Moses up into the mountain. In chapter 20 God gave Moses the Ten Commandments. In chapters 21-23 we have different judgments and laws which God gave to guide the people of Israel. In chapter 24 the elders of the nation agreed to keep God's covenant of law. Let us look at these chapters more carefully.

At Mount Sinai, chapter 19.

Three months after Israel had left Egypt they came to the desert of Sinai near the mountain of Sinai. Moses went up into the mountain and the Lord gave him a message for *"the house of Jacob.....*
the people of Israel," v.3. The first name of the father of the nation was Jacob. He learned many lessons from God and later God gave him a new name, Israel, Genesis 32.28. The house of Jacob and the people of Israel were the same, v.3. God had brought them out of Egypt and looked after them as a great bird carries its young birds. God's purpose was to draw them to Himself. If they would obey His voice they would be more precious to Him than all other nations. They would be a kingdom of priests and a holy nation.

We will soon see that Israel did not keep the Law of God, but these promises have been given to the Church. The Holy Spirit called the Christians holy priests, a chosen race, priests of the King, a holy nation, 1 Peter 2.5,9. We are also called a *"kingdom of priests,"* Revelation 1.6. God wants us to praise Him and tell others about His wonderful acts.

Moses came down from the mountain and called the leaders of the people together. The people did not know how weak they really were and quickly promised to keep God's Law, vs.7-9. The Lord told Moses that He would speak to him in a cloud. God wanted the people to know that He was really speaking to Moses.

Then the Lord told them to wash their clothes and be ready for the third day. They could come to the bottom of the mountain, but no one could touch the mountain. If anyone touched the mountain the other people had to put him to death without touch-

39

ing him. God was going to show them that He was holy and He wanted them to be pure in their bodies and in their hearts.

Then the great day came. There was a thick cloud on the mountain. Thunder and lightning came out of it. The loud noise of a trumpet made the people shake. Moses went up into the mountain, but God sent him down again. He told Moses to warn the people not to touch the mountain. Moses had already told the people about this and he thought that would be enough. The Lord knew the heart of man and told Moses to warn them again. Only Aaron could come up with Moses.

God sometimes used thunder and lightning to show His power. For example in the time of David, 1 Samuel 12.18; in the future judgment of the world, Revelation 4.5; 8.5; 11.19; 16.18.

If we know the love of God we do not need to be afraid of these things. The Lord always takes care of His children.

In the book of Hebrews we are taught that grace is better than law. The writer describes the fear of the people and of Moses himself at Mount Sinai. We have come to the true Mount Zion and the heavenly Jerusalem, to angels and saints, to God and to the Lord Jesus Christ. Those who refused the Law of Moses did not escape. Neither will those who turn from Christ today, Hebrews 12.18-26.

The Ten Commandments, chapter 20.

When Jehovah gave His Law to Israel He first told them again that He had brought them out of Egypt. Right away we see a great truth. God does not redeem a man because he knows or keeps the Law. God had already redeemed Israel out of Egypt. He redeems us through grace by the power of God and the blood of Christ.

Moses wrote these ten commands on stones, 34.28 .

1. God wants His people to love and worship Him. He will not allow them to worship other gods as well, v.3.

2. The Lord God is a jealous God. This means that He loves His people and wants their love for Himself. He told them not to make an image of anything whatever in the whole world. They must not bow down to any image or serve any false god. Bending the knees before an image shows that a man hates God. Those who do so teach their children and their children's children to do the same. God's judgment will be on the children as well. This does not mean that God punishes innocent children for the sins of their father. When the children follow their fathers God must punish the children as well. God's great work is showing mercy to the

thousands who love and obey Him, vs.4-6.

Bowing down before an image is the same as worshipping an idol. The New Testament warns us not to do it, 1 Corinthians 5.11; 6.9; 10.14; 2 Corinthians 6.16; Galatians 5.20; 1 John 5.21. Loving money is as bad as worshipping an idol, Ephesians 5.5, Colossians 3.5. These verses bring together the second and the tenth commandment.

3. The Lord told them not to take the name of God in vain, v.7. This means they should not break any promise made in the name of Jehovah. They should not lightly or carelessly use the name of Jehovah at any time.

We should not promise with an oath to do anything, Matthew 5.34-37, James 4.13-15; 5.12. We cannot know the future and can only promise to do something *if the Lord is willing.* Some people use the name of God very lightly as if God was an ordinary person. They should remember that God has all power and is a great King above all.

4. God had blessed the seventh day and made it different from the other days. He Himself rested from all His work on the seventh day, Genesis 2.3. He had already commanded Israel not to gather manna on the seventh day, Exodus 16.25,26. In the fourth commandment God told the people not to do any work at all on the seventh day. Children, servants and cattle should all rest.

Christians are not under law but under grace, Romans 6.14. We are not commanded to keep the sabbath day. We set aside the first day of the week to worship and serve the Lord. In this way the Christians have one day of rest out of seven. Even so keeping the first day of the week will not save you any more than keeping the sabbath day. God saves us not by our own deeds but by His mercy, Titus 3.5.

5. The fifth commandment is the first one with a promise, Ephesians 6.2,3. Those who honour their father and mother would have a long life in the land of promise, v.12. The Lord Jesus came to fulfil the law, Matthew 5.17. He obeyed the fifth commandment. When He was a boy He did what His parents told Him to do, Luke 2.51. At the time of His death He asked His beloved disciple John to look after His mother, John 19.26,27. The Pharisees tried to get around the fifth commandment. They told people they could give gifts to the temple instead of to their father and mother. The Lord Jesus showed that this was wrong. The Pharisees put the teaching of men on a higher level than the Word of God itself, Mark 7.9-13.

In Old Testament days God promised many blessings to those who obeyed Him. They would succeed in this world and live a long life. The Old Testament promises are not for us as Christians today. The promise of long life on this earth in Ephesians 6.3 shows the importance of the fifth commandment. Many young believers in these times have been killed because they were faithful to the Lord Jesus Christ. Certainly the Lord honoured Joseph and Mary completely, but His life on this earth was not long.

6-8. These three commands are against common sins which are considered wrong by most tribes and nations throughout the world. People who do these things are breaking God's law. The Lord Jesus made the laws for His kingdom still stronger. To think about sin in the heart is as bad as the actual sin, Matthew 5.21,22,27,28.

9. In the ninth commandment God told Israel not to say anything which is not true about another man or woman. We have seen in the third commandment we should not swear falsely in the name of the Lord. The first four commandments tell men what they should do in relation to God. The last six commandments are in relation to man. The first four can be put in short form in these words, *"You shall love the Lord your God with all your heart and with all your soul and with all your mind."* The second group of commandments can be put this way, *"You shall love your neighbour as yourself,"* Matthew 22.35-40, Deuteronomy 6.5, Leviticus 19.18.

God wants us to tell the truth. In both parts of the ten commandments He tells us not to say what is untrue. If I love my neighbour as myself I will not say anything untrue about him. The New Testament also teaches us not to lie, Ephesians 4.25, Colossians 3.9, Revelation 21.8. Christians should always practice the habit of telling the truth no matter what the results might be. God desires truth in the heart, Psalm 51.6. Ananias and his wife told Peter a lie. Ananias wanted the Christians to think that he had given everything to the Lord. Really he only gave part of his money. His wife Sapphira said the same thing. They were punished at once and died for their sin, Acts 5.1-11.

10. To covet means to want very badly something I do not have. God commanded His people not to covet anything belonging to another person. The tenth commandment is related to the seventh and eighth commandments because if I do not covet I will not take.

In some ways the tenth commandment is the hardest of the

six in the second part. This is because it has to do with the heart. The Lord wants us to give our hearts to Him and not to love the things of this world, neither our own things nor things belonging to someone else.

If God says anything once, all men should listen and obey. If He says it twice, we can see that it must be still more important. Moses gave these ten commandments again before Israel entered the land of promise, Deuteronomy 5.6-21. The second time they are in a little different form, but they mean the same thing.

The people heard the thunder and saw the lightning. They were afraid to stand close to the mountain. They did not want God to speak to them, but would listen to what He said through Moses, vs.18-20.

Moses drew near to the thick darkness where God was, vs.21-26. God explained more about the second commandment. The people had not seen God and so they could not make any image of silver or gold to look like God. All they needed to worship Him was an altar of earth. If they wanted to make an altar of stone, they should make it of uncut stones and without steps.

Why did God give the Law to Israel? The New Testament tells us that God will not say anyone is righteous because he keeps the law, Romans 3.20, Galatians 2.16; 3.11. Those who put themselves under law are under a curse. They will not be able to keep on doing all things which are written in the book of the law, Galatians 3.10. Why did God give the Law?

No one has ever kept the law of God perfectly except the Lord Jesus Christ. One time a young man asked the Lord what good thing he should do to have eternal life. The Lord Jesus told him to keep the commandments and love his neighbour as himself. The man thought he had done all these things ever since he was young. The Lord Jesus told him to sell all that he had and give the money to poor people. The young man was very rich and was not willing to obey. He must have known then that he did not love his neighbour as himself, Matthew 19.16-22.

We may say that the purpose of the law is to show man his great need of God's grace. Paul said he would not have known sin if it had not been for the law, Romans 7.7. The law is like a servant who takes his master's son to school. The purpose of the law is to show us that we are sinners and then to bring us to Christ, Galatians 3.24, Romans 5.20.

Those who believe in the Lord Jesus Christ should not walk

according to their natural desires, but according to the Holy Spirit. If they do they will keep God's commands as given in the law, Romans 8.4. Many verses teach us that we do not keep the law in order to be saved. When we are saved and know we are saved we want to please God. We want to do His will and to keep His commands, Romans 12.1,2. The Holy Spirit will help us in these things.

The judgments of Jehovah, chapters 21-23.

The ten commandments give us in short form what God required from His people. In chapters 21 to 23 God explained more fully some of these laws. He also added more rules for the life of the people of Israel. These chapters were to help Israel while they were in the wilderness and when they reached the promised land.

Slaves, 21.1-11.

Buying and selling people was a terrible practice of many nations years ago. A cruel master could make his slave work without pay. He could beat him or kill him if he would not work. Men, women and children taken captive in a war had to serve as slaves. The people of Israel used slaves also, but God's laws kept them from being as cruel as other nations.

If the people of Israel had obeyed God, no one would have been very poor. When anyone became poor and owed a lot of money, he could sell himself to someone and use the money to pay his debts. If a man of Israel bought a Hebrew slave he must let him go free after six years of work.

If the master gave his slave a wife, the slave might want to stay with his wife and family and not go out free again. He could say this plainly before the judges and his master would bore a hole through his ear. This would show that he belonged to his master forever. Here is a beautiful picture of Christ, the Servant of Jehovah. The Lord Jesus could have returned to heaven without dying. He loved His Bride, the Church of Christ and chose to be the Servant of God forever. He is now at God's right hand, but will be subject to God forever. God will be over all, 1 Corinthians 15.28.

If a girl was bought as a slave, she would not go out after six years, but stay in her master's house as his wife. If he was not kind to her, she could go out free, vs.7-11.

In the days of the Lord Jesus and His apostles many people bought and sold men as slaves. The Lord did not try to change this evil practice. The New Testament tells Christians to be kind and fair to all servants, Ephesians 6.9, Colossians 4.1. These commands make the practice of slavery less cruel.

It is not our business as Christians to fight against evil practices in this world such as slavery. Our God has commanded us to preach Christ. When the hearts of men are changed by faith in the Lord Jesus, they will be kind to others. There are many evil, unkind and unfair practices in the world around us. True Christians should spend their time and strength in obeying the command of the risen Christ. We are far from finishing the work which we were commanded to do. We should not spend even part of our lives doing other things which the Lord did not command us to do.

Violence, 21.12-36.

The sixth commandment says, *"You shall not kill."* Anyone who kills another must be put to death, vs.12-14. This was God's law since the time of Noah, Genesis 9.6. If the man did not **plan** to kill the other, then he could run to a city of refuge and he would be safe there. Later the Lord named six cities of refuge where men could run if they killed someone by accident. As long as the man stayed in the city of refuge, the brothers of the dead person could not kill him. If anyone hated another man and killed him, he would have to die. Even if he ran to the altar of Jehovah for safety, he could not be spared, 1 Kings 2.28.

The fifth law commands us to honour our father and mother. Anyone who struck or cursed father or mother would die for it, vs.15,17. Anyone who stole a man to sell him as a slave would have to die, v.16.

Then we find commands about punishing anyone who hurts someone else, vs.18-27. The general rule was, *"Eye for eye, tooth for tooth,"* v.24, Matthew 5.38. The judges will do to you just what you did to someone else.

The last part of the chapter, vs.28-35, deals with the case of an ox which hurts a person or another animal; also the case of someone falling into a hole. Whenever people live together, there will always be problems and quarrels. The written law helped the judges of Israel to decide on righteous punishment.

These verses teach us the perfect righteousness of God. As Christians we must obey the laws of the country in which we live. At times we may think that some of these laws are not very righteous. We must obey these laws and try to live a righteous life as Christians. When the Lord Jesus comes back, all laws and government will at last be righteous.

Private property, 22.1-15.

The eighth commandment says, *"You shall not steal."* If a man stole an animal, he would be punished, 22.1-4. A thief breaking into a man's house might get caught. If he was hurt, he could not make the man of the house pay him anything. Even if he died the man of the house was not to be punished. If he followed the thief in anger and killed him, then he would be guilty.

If a man should let his animal eat grass on another man's land, he would have to pay for it, v.5. If he started a fire which burned another man's grain, he would have to pay for it, v.6. If a man asked his neighbour to look after something and it was stolen, the thief would have to pay up. If the thief was not found, it might be thought that the man had taken it himself. In this case they would bring the man before God to find out the truth, vs.7-13. If anyone borrowed something from his neighbour he must return it or pay for it, vs.14,15.

You can see that these laws are fair and righteous. Behind them all was this, *"You shall love your neighbour as yourself."*

More judgments and laws, 22.16 - 23.19.

In these verses we have many different laws which explain more clearly the ten commandments. We also read how the judges would punish the person who broke God's laws.

If a man lies with a girl it is a sin. If she had not promised to marry anyone else, the man must take her as his wife. If her father is not willing for them to get married, then the man must pay money for his sin, vs.16,17.

The people of Israel must put to death anyone who talks with evil spirits, v.18; anyone who lies with an animal, v.19; and anyone who worships a false god, v.20.

The Holy Spirit showed Paul that many will listen to wicked spirits in later times, 1 Timothy 4.1. This terrible sin is becoming more common today. It is not our duty as Christians to kill people for any sin. We should pray for them and try to keep others from following their evil ways.

The Lord commanded the people of Israel to be kind to the poor, specially to widows or children without a father. If any man made trouble for these poor people, God would take away his life. In this way his wife would become a widow and his children be without a father, vs.21-24.

If a person became poor, and had to borrow some money, the one who lent the money must be kind to the poor man, vs.25-27. No one should say an evil thing about God nor about the rulers of Israel, v.28. The apostle Paul thought of this verse after he had spoken with anger in the council, Acts 23.5.

We have seen that the first-born of man and animals belonged to Jehovah. Part of every harvest also belonged to the Lord, vs.29,30. A young animal could stay with its mother for seven days.

The people of Israel were not to eat the meat of an animal which a wild animal had killed, v.31.

God commanded His people to tell the truth, specially in a court. They should not follow the crowd and do what was wrong just because everybody else was doing it, 23.1,2. In deciding a case they must judge fairly both the rich, v.3, and the poor, vs.6,7. A judge should not accept a gift from anyone, v.8. People should be kind to those who hate them, vs.4,5, and to strangers, v.9.

Special days and years, 23.10-19.

God commanded Israel to plant their land and gather their crops for six years, Leviticus 25.1-7. In the seventh year they should neither plant nor gather crops. Any food that grew of itself was for the poor people and wild animals, vs.10,11. The seventh day of every week was for rest, v.12. They should listen to God's commands and not even speak the names of false gods, v.13.

There were to be three feasts every year, vs.14-19. God had already commanded them to keep the feast of unleavened bread, 12.14-17. They should also keep two other feasts, one at the beginning of the harvest and the other at the end of the harvest. The feast at the end of the harvest is called the *feast of booths,* Deuteronomy 16.13. There were in all seven feasts of Jehovah, Leviticus 23, but every man had to go before the Lord three times every year.

At the time of the Passover they should use unleavened bread and burn the fat of the lamb, v.18, Numbers 18.17. The first grain ready to eat should be brought to the house of the Lord for the priests. The people of Israel should not boil a baby goat in its mother's milk as the people of Canaan did, v.19; 34.26, Deuteronomy 14.21.

Which of these commands must be obeyed by Christians today? To answer this question we must see the difference between two kinds of laws. Some laws have to do with the tabernacle and worship in Old Testament days. These laws have been fulfilled

47

in Christ and are not put on us today. For example Israel had to bring many animals as sacrifices to God. These animals were pictures of the Lord Jesus Christ in His death. Since Christ has died for us we do not need to bring animal sacrifices to God, Hebrews 10.12.

Other laws tell us to love God and man. Many of these are found again in the New Testament. The Holy Spirit gives us both the desire and the power to keep these laws. These are called moral laws. Commands concerning worship in the tabernacle are called ceremonial laws. Keeping the law will not take away our sins nor take us to heaven, Titus 3.5.

Some of these commands told the people of Israel how to punish those who did wrong. These were necessary for a nation like Israel. As Christians we should obey the laws of our own government, Romans 13.1-7, Titus 3.1, 1 Peter 2.13-15.

Blessings for those who obey God, 23.20-33.

God promised that His Angel would go with the people of Israel. If they obeyed God they would get the victory over their enemies. God would give them the land of Canaan and they would drive out the wicked men who lived there. They must never worship the gods of these nations, v.24, nor make any agreement with the people, v.32.

God promised that their victory over their enemies would be certain but not sudden, vs.29,30. In the Christian life we sometimes are sad because the old sinful habits do not go away at once. Satan tempts us again and again and leads us into sin. However by looking to the Lord we can grow stronger and become more like Him.

Some Old Testament promises are not for Christians. People in Israel who obeyed God's commands could expect to succeed and be in good health, vs.25,26. God has promised us to supply our needs, to give us food and clothing and to answer prayer. Our blessings are spiritual blessings, Ephesians 1.3.

The Blood Covenant, chapter 24.

After saying these things God told Moses to bring a few men to the mountain. God named Aaron and two of his sons, Nadab and Abihu, 6.23, and Moses could choose 70 others of the leaders of Israel. One of these was Joshua, v.13. Of these only Moses could come near. The others should worship from far off.

When Moses came down from the mountain he told the people

all that God had commanded him, vs.3-8. These people did not know how weak they really were. They quickly promised to do everything that God had commanded. Moses wrote all these words of Jehovah in a book, v.4; 17.14, Deuteronomy 31.9. The people could not forget God's written law, but Moses knew that they would not keep it. He built an altar at the foot of the mountain and the young men offered sacrifices. Moses put some blood on the altar, some on the people and some on the book itself, Hebrews 9.19. The people understood that they would die if they did not obey God's command.

Then the 74 men went up the mountain and they saw a glorious appearance of God. The Lord had specially commanded that no one could come up the mountain, 19.12,13,21-24. Now a sacrifice had been made and the Lord told these men they could come up and be safe. They did not see the very form of God, Deuteronomy 4.12. No man, not even Moses, could see God's face and live, 33.20, 1 Timothy 6.16. Whatever we can know of God is seen in His Son, John 1.18.

Then Moses and Joshua went up the mountain again, vs.12-14. God promised to write the commands on tables of stone and give them to Moses.

The glory of the Lord was on Mount Sinai for six days. On the seventh day God spoke again to Moses, vs.15-18. Moses was in a cloud which looked like fire to the people of Israel further down. Moses and Joshua were in the mountain for 40 days and 40 nights before they came down again, 32.15. While they were there God told them about the tabernacle and the priests, chapters 25-31.

The people of Israel could not go up the mountain and Moses could go near to God only by special command. From these things we learn how holy God is. Now that Christ has died for us and risen again from the dead, we are able to go in and be near to God at all times. The work of the Lord Jesus Christ is a perfect work. Even sinful men who are washed in His blood can come before God and worship Him without fear, Hebrews 10. 19-22.

Lesson 6
HOW TO BUILD THE TABERNACLE, chapters 25-27.

God had delivered His people from the land of Egypt. They had been slaves to Pharaoh, but God redeemed them by blood and by power. Israel had seen God's hand supplying their needs in the desert and given them victory over their enemies. God had given them His commands and judgments and the people of Israel had promised to obey, 24.3. Now the redeemed people were ready to worship God. True, they sang God's praise when He had destroyed their enemies, chapter 15, but the tabernacle with its sacrifices and priests gave Israel a way to worship God at any time. The tabernacle was also necessary for a failing sinful nation. Although Israel had promised to obey God's law, He knew that they would often sin against Him. The tabernacle with its sacrifices and priests were the plan of a holy God to keep a failing nation before Him.

Commands about the **sacrifices** are found in the first few chapters of the book of Leviticus. The rest of Exodus gives us:

1. Commands for the tabernacle and the priests,
   chapters 25-31.
2. The sin of Israel, chapters 32-34.
3. The building of the tabernacle, chapters 35-40.

The tabernacle was a tent set up in a courtyard which had curtains around it. In the courtyard there were two objects: an **altar** where the priests made sacrifices, and a **laver** where they washed their hands and their feet. The tent was in two parts, the front one twice as big as the other. The front part was called the Holy Place and in it were three objects: a table, a lampstand, and a small altar. The other part of the tent was called the Most Holy Place. In it there was nothing but the **ark**. We will read about these objects in the following order:

Chapter 25 - the ark, the table and the lampstand.
Chapter 26 - the tent.
Chapter 27 - the bronze altar and the court.
Chapter 28 - the priests' clothing.
Chapter 29 - the priests are given to God.
Chapter 30 - the gold altar and the laver.

The children of Israel had worked for many years in Egypt without pay. When God judged the Egyptians they were glad to see the Israelites go. The Egyptians were willing to give the people of Israel whatever they needed, 12.35,36. Now the Lord said that the people of Israel could give something to Him for the building of the

50

tabernacle, 25.1-9. The command to give was only to those who really wanted in their own hearts to give to the Lord. A list of the materials needed is given in verses 3-7. God was going to show Moses how to make the tabernacle and everything that was in it. The people could give metal, v.3; white linen cloth and different colours, v.4; goat's hair and skins of animals, vs.4,5; wood, v.5; oil, v.6; valuable stones, v.7.

The tabernacle made a way for Israel to come to God. For this reason the tabernacle speaks of the Lord Jesus Christ who alone can say, *"I am the way....no one comes to the Father but by me,"* John 14.6. The tabernacle is God's picture book. Almost everything in it speaks of Christ. Everything in the tabernacle has a spiritual meaning and some of these meanings are easy enough to understand. Some of the materials were used to make several things in the tabernacle; others were used only once. We read of some of these materials in other parts of the Bible as well. Many Bible teachers feel that some of these materials have certain meanings. We will explain these meanings as we study things made of the different materials.

Gold   — the glory of God
Silver   — redemption
Brass (bronze) —   judgment
Blue   — heaven
Purple   — a king
Scarlet   — suffering
Fine linen   — the perfect righteousness of Christ
Acacia wood— Christ as a Man

The ark, 25.10-22.

The ark was a box made of wood and covered with gold. The size of the ark is given in verse 10. A cubit is about 18 inches, so the ark was about 45 inches long, 27 inches wide and 27 inches high. The acacia wood was covered with pure gold inside and out. There were four rings of gold, one for each corner. Moses was to make two long poles of wood and cover them with gold. Each pole went through two rings so the priests could carry the ark. The ark was called the **ark of the testimony** because the commands and testimonies of God were put in it. Later on Moses and Aaron put the gold pot of manna and Aaron's rod in the ark, 16.33, Numbers 17.10, Hebrews 9.4.

The top of the ark was a thin piece of gold the same size as the box. This top was made of pure gold. From the same piece of gold

51

The Ark of Jehovah

The Altar of Incense

they made the shape of two angels or cherubim. These were placed at each end of the mercy seat, the top of the ark. The two angels faced each other looking down toward the mercy seat with their wings spread out.

The mercy seat was the place where God met with Moses and talked with him. In this way the ark was a sign that Jehovah was with His people. The cherubim are angels who guard the righteousness of God. When God put Adam and Eve out of the garden of Eden, the cherubim with a flaming sword kept the way of the tree of life, Genesis 3.24. On the ark the cherubim looked down on the mercy seat where God's mercy flowed out to His people. The testimony of the law inside the ark was against the sinning people, but this was covered by the mercy seat. On the day of atonement the high priest put the blood of a sacrifice on the mercy seat, Leviticus 16.14. The cherubim above were watching all this.

God can never show mercy by setting aside His righteousness. His mercy and righteousness must go together. Here we see that the cherubim and the mercy seat were made of one piece of gold. The righteousness and mercy of God cannot be separated. How can God be both righteous and merciful at the same time? Only because of the work of Christ on the cross. God must punish sin and His Son has paid the price. The blood was shed. Now God can show mercy to all who believe. The mercy seat in the tabernacle is a beautiful picture of this.

The Lord Jesus Christ is called Emmanuel, which means God with us, Matthew 1.23, and the ark is a picture of Christ. The Lord Jesus Christ was both God and Man. The ark was made of common wood covered with pure gold. The gold speaks of the glory of God and the acacia wood speaks of Christ as a Man. The righteousness and mercy of God met together in Christ. Only on this ground can God meet man. These are some of the lessons of the ark.

The ark made Israel sure that God was with them. Many years later the nation broke God's laws and God had to punish them. When their enemies came against them, they thought that God would help them. The priests took the ark to the battle, but the enemies won the victory and took the ark, 1 Samuel 4.11. God will never bless His people while they go on in their sins.

The table for the bread, 25.23-30.

The table of the bread was also made of wood covered with gold. It was as high as the ark, but shorter and narrower, 36 inches long,

18 inches wide and 27 high. The table had an ornament of gold on all four sides near the top. In this way it was like the ark, v.11, and the gold altar, 30.3. The table also had a frame on all four sides which would keep the bread from slipping off when the table was moved, Numbers 4.7. The table, the ark and the two altars had rings and poles so the priests or Levites could carry them. There were also golden bowls and other dishes of different shapes, all made of pure gold, v.29. The dishes were used for incense or frankincense, Leviticus 24.7. **Flagons** or large cups, and bowls, were used for the wine offerings, 29.40, Numbers 15.5,7,10. The bread and wine make us think of the Lord's supper, 1 Corinthians 11.23, 25. The gold table was called the table of the bread of the **Presence**, because it spoke of the presence of Jehovah.

The ark and the table and the small altar were all made of wood covered with gold. They all speak of the Lord Jesus Christ, the God-Man in different ways. Twelve loaves of bread were set on the table of the Presence, Leviticus 24.5,6. These twelve loaves speak of the twelve tribes of Israel as **one nation**. The table of the Presence speaks of Christ holding up the people of God in their oneness before God. Later the nation was divided, but in God's sight they were all His people, one people, Ezekiel 37.16,17.

Today also God thinks of His people as one. The Lord Jesus prayed that they all might be one, John 17.11, and God always answers the prayers of His Son, John 11.42. Christians today are divided into many different churches, but true believers are all one in Christ, Ephesians 4.4, Galatians 3.28. There is no need to form a system of churches. True believers **are** one in Christ. Unbelievers can enter the true church only by believing in Christ.

The gold lampstand, 25.31-40.

The lampstand was made of pure gold and weighed about 94 lbs. It had a center stem with three branches going out of each side. The centre stem and each branch had a lamp, seven lamps in all. There were no windows in the tabernacle and the only light was from the lampstand in the holy place. In the most holy place there was no light at all. The Lord said that He would live in darkness, 1 Kings 8.12. The snuffers and trays were also made of pure gold, v.38. The high priest used these to keep the lamps clean and burning brightly. The people brought pure olive oil and the lamps were burning all the time, Leviticus 24.2-4.

Today all true Christians are priests, 1 Peter 2.5,9, and we need both food and light. The table of bread and the lampstand

The Table for the Bread

The Gold Lampstand

both speak of the Lord Jesus Christ. Just as God is light, 1 John 1.5, so the Lord Jesus could say, *"I am the light of the world; he who follows me will not walk in darkness, but will have the light of life,"* John 8.12. Christ is also the Bread of Life, John 6.35. The Lord also taught His disciples *"You are the light of the world,"* Matthew 5.14. The gold lampstand was inside the tabernacle, but it spoke of the nation of Israel showing to the world the truth of God. Today this is our work. The Lord Jesus saw the seven churches as seven gold candlesticks, Revelation 1.20.

God spoke to Moses and told him how to build the tabernacle and everything in it. He also showed Moses a plan, 25.9,40; 26.30; 27.8, Numbers 8.4, Acts 7.44. The tabernacle was a copy of heavenly things, Hebrews 8.5.

We do not build tabernacles and church buildings today after some plan found in the Bible. The Church of God is a group of Christians who have been born again. It is very important that every servant of God should build up churches according to the plan in the New Testament, 1 Corinthians 3.10.

Coverings for the tent, 26.1-14.

The two side walls and the back of the tabernacle were made of boards. Coverings were put over these boards. The first of these coverings were the curtains made of fine linen, blue, purple and scarlet with figures of cherubim. There were ten curtains, each one 28 cubits by 4 cubits, that is, 42 feet long and six feet wide. The curtains went across the top of the tabernacle and hung down the walls to within one cubit of the ground. The curtains were held together by blue string and gold wire, vs.1-6.

These beautiful curtains speak in a wonderful way of our Lord Jesus Christ. Fine linen speaks of righteousness, Revelation 19.8, and so of the perfect human life of the Lord. Blue is the colour of the sky and so it makes us think of the Son of God who came down from heaven. Purple is a colour often worn by kings, Judges 8.26. Our Lord Jesus Christ came as the King of Israel and will come back again to be King over the whole world. *Scarlet* however speaks of suffering. Scarlet colour was made by crushing a small creeping thing or a worm. To get scarlet colour a living thing had to give its life. In Psalm 22.6 we can hear the voice of the Lord Jesus saying, *"I am a worm and no man."* This is the scarlet worm or creeping thing from which scarlet colour was made. The curtains of the tabernacle show us four sides of our Lord's life.

It is interesting to see that each of these four is important in one of the four Gospels. John shows Christ as the Son of God; Luke as the perfect Son of Man. In Mark we see the suffering Servant of Jehovah and Matthew tells us of Christ as the King.

Blue	Linen	Scarlet	Purple
John	Luke	Mark	Matthew
The Son of God	The Perfect Man	The Suffering Servant	The King

On top of these beautiful curtains in the tabernacle were laid eleven curtains of goat's hair. These were two cubits longer than the linen curtains and so just reached to the ground on both sides.

The goats' hair curtains were joined together by brass wire, vs. 11-14. These curtains were the same width as the linen curtains, but there were eleven of them instead of only ten. The first curtain was partly doubled back over the front of the tabernacle and the last one reached a little beyond the back of the tabernacle, vs.9, 12. On top of the goat's hair curtains were laid two leather coverings, one of rams' skins and the other of goats' skins, v.14. These were to keep the rain from getting through the linen curtains to the tabernacle below.

People outside the tabernacle could not see the beautiful curtains which speak of our Saviour. These curtains were covered by the rough goats' hair curtains and by the two leather coverings. So it is with the Lord Jesus. Unsaved people cannot see any beauty in our blessed Lord. For them He is like "a root out of a dry ground" without form or beauty," Isaiah 53.2. Those of us who have come to know Him see Him as the Bride saw her Beloved. To us Christ is the chief among ten thousand and most lovely, Song of Solomon 5.10,16.

The frames of the tabernacle, 26.15-30.

Fifty frames of acacia wood covered with gold were used for the three walls of the tabernacle. These were on the south, the west and the north sides. These frames were ten cubits high and 1½ cubits wide, that is 15 ft. x 27 inches. There were 20 frames for each side, vs.18-20. From this we learn that the tabernacle was 30 cubits or 45 ft. long. At the back of the tabernacle there were six frames and two special frames for the corners. It would seem that the tabernacle was ten cubits wide. In Solomon's temple the most holy place was 20 cubits long, 20 cubits wide and 20 cubits high, 1 Kings 6.20. No doubt this was the same shape as the most holy place of the tabernacle. We know that in the tabernacle the most

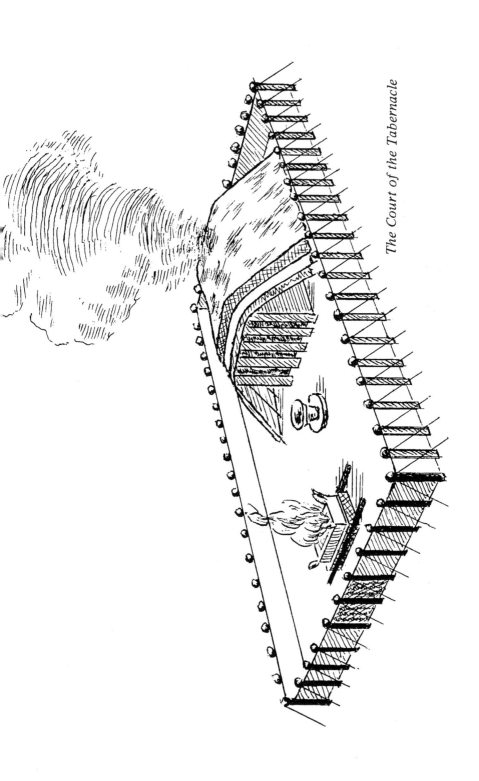

The Court of the Tabernacle

holy place was ten cubits high and it could have been ten cubits long and ten cubits wide as well. This would mean that the veil between the holy place and the most holy place was ten cubits from the back of the tabernacle and twenty cubits from the front.

The frames of the tabernacle were made of wood covered with gold. Wood speaks of the nature of man and gold speaks of the glory of God. We have seen that these two materials suggest the person of our Lord Jesus Christ, the God-Man. In the tabernacle however there were many frames and these may speak of believers in Christ. Do we have two natures? Yes. Like all men we are born with the nature of Adam. When we are born again we share in God's nature, 2 Peter 1.4. We should put off the old nature, Colossians 3.9, but we do not completely lose it until the Lord comes. Then we will be changed into His likeness, 1 John 3.2. We will never lose the new nature. In the frames of the tabernacle the gold was on the outside and people could not see the natural wood. In the same way we should show the people around us the new nature which we have from God. Again, these frames in the tabernacle were used to hold up the beautiful curtains, a picture of the Lord Jesus Christ. So we as believers hold up Christ before the world and do not seek for our own glory.

The frames of the tabernacle stood on silver bases and were held together at the top by gold rings. Jehovah also told Moses to make 15 rods of wood and cover them with gold. These rods were also used to keep the frames in place. The gold rings speak of God the Holy Spirit. The Holy Spirit joins many believers into one Building, the Temple of God today, Ephesians 2.21,22. The gold bars also speak of us as believers with two natures. We are not told to make the Church one, but to keep the oneness which the Spirit makes, Ephesians 4.3,16.

The bases were made of silver, and the frames stood in these bases. We shall see that this silver speaks of redemption, 30.11-16; 38.27. The frames could not stand by themselves without the silver bases. We cannot do any service for the Lord unless we understand that He has redeemed us.

The veils, 26.31-37.

There were two veils or curtains for the tabernacle. One divided the Holy Place from the Most Holy Place. The other hung on the east side where there was no wall. The ark with the mercy seat was put in the Most Holy Place, v.34. The table was set on the north side of the Holy Place, the lampstand on the south side. As the priest entered the Holy Place, he would see the table on his right hand and the lampstand on his left. Both of the veils were probably ten cubits wide and ten cubits high. They were both made of linen with blue and purple and scarlet stuff. The inner veil had figures of cherubim worked into it like the ten curtains. The inner veil was held up by gold hooks and four pillars or columns. The pillars were made of acacia wood covered with gold. These pillars stood in bases of silver.

The curtains or screen for the front of the tabernacle was held up by gold hooks, v.37. This screen was held up by five pillars made of wood and covered with gold. The pillars stood in bases of brass. The people of Israel entered the court of the tabernacle and could see the screen at the front, but they could not go into the tabernacle. The priests could go inside and could see the beauty of the inner veil and also the inside of the curtain across the top. All these were made of the same material.

Both of these veils speak of Christ as the Way to enter into the presence of God. We have seen that the four materials used in the curtains and the veils speak of Christ in four different ways. When the Lord Jesus died for our sins the inside veil was torn from the top to the bottom, Matthew 27.51. As believers we are priests of God and we can enter into the Most Holy Place through the veil which has been torn. Indeed the Holy Spirit commands us to enter without fear, Hebrews 10.19-22. God has put away our sins forever. Now we are able to stand before God without fear and worship Him who has done so much for us.

The brass altar, 27.1-8.

When a man entered the court of the tabernacle the first thing he would see was the brass altar. Sacrifices which had been offered to Jehovah were burned on this altar.

Many thousands of animals were sacrificed to God on the brass altar. These were only a covering for sin for a short time. No man can come to God without a blood sacrifice, but the blood of animals can never take away sin. Those animals spoke of Christ who indeed can take all our sin away, Hebrews 10.4, 12.

This altar was made of acacia wood and covered with brass. It was five cubits long and five cubits wide, 7½ feet each way. It was 3 cubits or 4½ ft. high. On each corner was a horn. The horns of an animal are the sign of its strength. Part of the blood of the sacrifices was put on the horns of the altar, 29.12. A person in danger could run to the altar and take hold of the horns, 1 Kings 1.50,51. With the altar there were pots for the ashes, a net, and other things made of brass. The altar was carried by two rods or poles made of wood and covered with brass. These were put into the brass rings at the corners of the altar.

The brass altar speaks of Christ bearing the judgment of God for our sins. This is the first truth the sinner must learn in coming to God. Unless he has a Sacrifice which God can accept, the sinner could never come near. Praise God we have such a Sacrifice in our Lord Jesus Christ!

The court of the tabernacle, 27.9-19.

The court of the tabernacle had curtains on four sides. The curtains were made of fine linen and held up by brass pillars and silver hooks. The pillars were set in bases of brass. The court was 100 cubits long and 50 cubits wide, 150 ft. by 75 ft. On the east side there was a gate 20 cubits wide. The hanging for the gate was made of fine linen with blue, purple and scarlet colour. This hanging was held up by silver hooks, and four brass pillars standing in brass bases.

Only Israelites could enter the court of the tabernacle. Other people from the outside could see the fine linen which speaks of the Lord Jesus as a Man. Today many people think of Christ only as a great Man and Teacher. If the people outside the tabernacle looked more closely they might see the brass pillars and the silver hooks. The altar of judgment was made of brass and so brass speaks of judgment. We have seen that silver speaks of redemption. If people today see themselves as sinners under judgment, they could learn that God has given them a Redeemer.

Anyone who tried to enter into the presence of God would have to come to the front gate of the tabernacle. There he would see the beautiful curtain and learn more of the beauties of Christ. If he believed and entered, he would learn more and more about the Lord. These are some of the lessons of the tabernacle.

Oil for the lamp, 27.20,21.

God also told Moses that Israel should bring pure olive oil for the lamps in the tabernacle. Aaron and his sons had to keep these lamps burning day and night. This light is like God's truth. It must never stop shining. Even when everything seems dark around us, we must shine as lights for the Lord, Ephesians 5.8.

LESSON 7
MORE ABOUT HOW TO BUILD THE TABERNACLE,
chapters 28-34.

In the New Testament we find that both Moses and Aaron are pictures of the Lord Jesus Christ. Our Lord is called the Apostle and High Priest of our confession, Hebrews 3.1-6. The word apostle means *one who is sent*. It refers to Moses as the one whom God sent to deliver His people from Egypt. Moses did not want to go alone, so God called Aaron to help him, Exodus 4.14. Now we read that God called Aaron and his sons to serve as priests. Later Aaron's son took Aaron's place and was called the high priest, Numbers 35.25. In Exodus 28 we learn how the priests' clothing was to be made and in chapter 29 how Aaron and his sons were consecrated for the office of priest.

The clothing of the high priest, 28.1-39.

The holy clothes for Aaron were for glory and beauty, v.2. Some of the Israelites were given special skill from the Lord and were called to make Aaron's clothing. There were six pieces of clothing for the high priest. All of them were made of fine linen. Some had blue, purple and scarlet colour just like the curtains and veils of the tabernacle. Gold was also used in Aaron's clothing, v.6.

The ephod, 28.5-14.

The ephod was in two parts, one for the back and one for the front. These parts were joined at the shoulders and held around the middle of the body by a girdle. On each shoulder piece was a precious onyx stone. On each onyx stone the names of six tribes were written. Onyx stone was found in the land of Havilah, Genesis 2.11,12. Solomon used it in the temple, 1 Chronicles 29.2. The onyx stone was also used as the eleventh stone in the breast piece, v.20. It may have been engraved with the name of Jacob's eleventh son, Joseph.

The breast piece, outside the ephod, 28.15-29.

The breast piece was made of the same materials as the ephod, about 8 inches square. Twelve precious stones were set in the ephod, each one with the name of a tribe of Israel, vs.17-21. The breast piece was supported on the shoulders of the high priest with gold chains. It was held tightly to the ephod with gold rings.

The names of the tribes of Israel were on the shoulders and the heart of the high priest, vs.11,29. The shoulder is the place of strength and the heart is the place of love. In the same way our Great High Priest has the power and the love to keep our names always before God.

One day a sick man came to the Lord Jesus. He knew that the Lord was able to make him better, but he was not sure if He would be willing to do so. The sick man soon found that the Lord had both **power** and **love**, Mark 1.40-42.

Urim and Thummim, 28.30.

These words mean *"lights and perfections."* It is thought that they were precious stones which the high priest used to find out the will of God. For example, when David wanted to know God's will, he told the priest to bring the ephod, 1 Samuel 23.9; 30.7. The word judgment in the *"breast piece of judgment"* does not mean God's anger, but what He decides on any matter. For ourselves we can say that our names are near the heart of Christ. He will guide us by showing us the will of God at all times.

The blue robe, 28.31-35.

Under the ephod the high priest wore a blue robe which was made all in one piece. The design of pomegranate fruit was worked into the bottom of the robe in blue and purple and scarlet. Between the pomegranates was hung a little bell made of gold. Every time the high priest took a step while wearing this robe, the bells would make a little sound. When Aaron went into the Holy Place, the people outside could hear the sound of the bells. They would know that the high priest had not died in the presence of Jehovah. This also teaches us how careful we must be when standing before a holy God.

The turban, 28.36-38.

The high priest's duty was very important. The turban on his head shows this once more. On the front of the turban was a plate of pure gold with these words on it "HOLY TO JEHOVAH." Aaron's duty was to see that all the sacrifices were made according to God's law.

The Lord Jesus Christ can act as our Great High Priest because of His death for us, Hebrews 9.12. He is a Priest whose life will never end, Hebrews 7.16. He is quite able to look after the people of God today.

The coat and the girdle, 28.39.

The coat was, like the turban, made out of fine linen. The beautiful girdle or belt kept Aaron's clothing close to the middle of his body.

The clothing of the other priests, 28.40-43.

Aaron's sons the priests also wore special clothing of linen, 39.27. The priests had to wear these clothes at all times when they came before the Lord. Aaron too had linen clothes which he wore on the day of atonement, Leviticus 16.23. The priests had to wear linen clothes next to their skin, vs.42,43.

Today some men say they are priests in a special way. They wear special clothes so everybody will know who they are. We have seen that *all* true believers today are priests, 1 Peter 2.5,9. We should be known by our good works, not by special clothing.

How the priests should be anointed, chapter 29.

In chapter 29 we have the anointing of the priests, vs.1-9; the sacrifices which were offered at the same time, vs.10-28; Aaron's clothing to be put on his son after Aaron died, vs.29,30; seven days of consecration, vs.31-37; and the daily burnt offering, vs.38-46.

Before Aaron or his sons could serve as priests they had to be anointed and consecrated. The Lord commanded Moses to take a young bull and two rams and bread without yeast. The animals had to be perfect and some of the bread had oil mixed in it or on top of it. Aaron and his sons were washed with water at the door of the tent, then Moses was to put their clothing on them. Moses also was to anoint Aaron by pouring a little oil on his head, v.7. He did the same to the sons, v.21. Then Aaron's four sons were clothed in their linen clothes, vs.8,9.

The priests were washed with water at the beginning of their service for the Lord. In the same way we are washed clean when we are born again, Titus 3.5. This washing is by the Word of God, 1 Peter 1.23. We will see that the priests had to wash their hands and feet with water whenever they came into the tabernacle, 30.17-21. We believers are walking every day in this world and cannot help getting the dirt of this world on our feet. Reading the Word of God every day will help to keep us clean. We also ought to wash one another's feet, John 13.10,14. We do this by teaching the Word of God to one another. This helps to keep us clean in God's sight.

Moses brought in the young bull as a sin offering for the priests. Aaron and his sons put their hands on the head of the young bull vs.10-14. This was to show that they were connected with their offering. They should have died for their own sin, but the sacrifice died instead of them. Moses put some of the blood on the horns of the altar and poured out the rest at the bottom of the altar. He burned some of the animal on the altar and the rest outside the camp.

Moses sacrificed one of the rams as a burnt offering, vs.15-18. He cut it in pieces, then burned the whole animal on the altar. When he killed the other ram, vs.19-21, he put a little of the blood on the priests on three parts of their bodies. Then he put both blood and oil on the priests and their clothing. This made them holy to the Lord.

We hear with our ears, we do things with our hands, and go places with our feet. We should use these parts of our body and the whole body for the Lord alone, Romans 12.1,2.

Moses burned the fat on the altar, vs.13,22. The fat was considered to be the best part of the animal. The people of Israel gave the fat to Jehovah and burned it on the altar. God told the people of Israel not to eat the fat, Leviticus 7.23-25.

Moses put parts of the ram on the hands of Aaron and his sons, also some of the bread. This was for a "wave offering", vs.22-25. While holding these things the priest moved his hands from side to side. He was offering this sacrifice to the God of the whole world who is everywhere. All was then burned on the altar.

Part of this offering was given to Moses, vs.26-28. Part of it was given to Aaron and his sons. God commanded that part of the sacrifices of the people of Israel was always to be given to Aaron and the priests.

In Leviticus we will learn more about the sacrifices, but there are many things which we do not fully understand. The main thing is that all these sacrifices speak of the Lord Jesus Christ in His death. From the rules for the priests we should learn that everything belongs to God.

The Lord commanded that one of Aaron's sons should become high priest after Aaron died. The son would use the same holy clothes, vs.29,30.

Under the Law no man could become a priest unless he was born into the family of Aaron. Today it is the same. Only those who are born into the family of God can serve God as true priests. There is nothing in the New Testament about taking certain young men, giving them higher education, then making them priests different from all the rest of God's people.

It took a full week for the consecration of Aaron and his sons, vs.31-37. Sacrifices were offered every day and the priests had to eat part of the sacrifice for that day. If any was left over they had to burn it with fire. No one else could eat any of it. Every day they offered a bull as a sin offering. The sacrifices of this week also made the altar most holy. Anything that touched the altar belonged to Jehovah. In all these things God was teaching Israel that He was holy. We should learn the same lessons.

Every day the priests had to offer two lambs on the altar, one in the morning and one in the evening. Along with the lamb there were offerings of flour, of oil and of wine.

We Christians are not under Law but we would do well to follow this example. It is a good thing for a Christian to have a quiet time with the Lord and worship God every morning and every evening. The lamb for the daily offering was completely burnt on the altar. This speaks of the Lord Jesus who gave His life completely to God. The fine flour speaks of His sinless life, because no evil whatever was found in Him. The oil is a picture of the Holy Spirit who was given to Christ without measure, John 3.34. Wine often speaks of joy in the Bible and in the New Testament wine makes us think of the blood of Christ, 1 Corinthians 11.25. As we think about the Lord Jesus, His perfect life and wonderful death, we should thank God for Him. This is our daily worship.

God also saw in the daily burnt offering a picture of His blessed Son. He promised to meet with the people of Israel and to put His glory on the tabernacle, vs.42-46. He would be their God and dwell among them. The Lord Jesus also promised that God would dwell in the hearts of those who love Him and obey Him, John 14.15, 16,21,23. These verses speak of God the Father, God the Son and God the Holy Spirit.

More furnishings for the tabernacle, chapter 30.

We have seen that the Lord told Moses how to make the ark, the table and the lamp stand in chapter 25, and the bronze altar, 27.1-8. Now we will read of the altar of incense, vs.1-10, and the laver, vs.17-21.

The altar of incense, 30.1-10.

After God commanded Moses to anoint the priests, He told him how to make the gold altar of incense. This was made of acacia wood, one cubit or 18 inches square at the top and two cubits or three feet high. It was covered with gold and had four horns at the four corners. It had also an ornament round about it and two rings. Wooden rods covered with gold were put through these two rings so the priests could carry the altar.

The altar of incense stood in the Holy Place in front of the veil. Every morning and every evening Aaron had to clean the lamps on the gold lampstand. At the same time he was to put incense on the gold altar. Every year on the day of atonement he put a little blood on the horns of the gold altar, Leviticus 16.18.

The priests could not burn any animal sacrifice or any meal offering on the gold altar, v.9. It was used only for burning incense. The gold altar speaks of the Lord Jesus as Man and God. He is our great High Priest who offers our praises to God. Aaron and all his sons could serve as priests only until they died. As the God-Man the Lord Jesus is a priest after the order of Melkizedek. Now He lives forever to pray for His own people, Hebrews 7.25. The gold altar has to do with **prayer**. Zechariah the priest burned incense in the temple when the people were outside praying, Luke 1.9,10. See also Revelation 8.3,4. Like the daily burnt offering the gold altar teaches us that we should pray to the Lord every day.

The atonement money, 30.11-16.

Next the Lord gave a command about numbering the people of Israel. Whenever the people were counted every man who was 20 years old or more should pay half a shekel as an offering to the Lord. Rich people could not give more for this purpose and the poor could not give less than half a shekel. We will see that animals were sacrificed to make atonement, Leviticus 1.4; 4.20,26; 9.7. These animals speak of Christ. The half shekel was a piece of silver. It also speaks of the redemption which Christ Jesus gives us.

We know that we are not redeemed by paying silver or gold, 1 Peter 1.18. The atonement money speaks of the price which **Christ** paid to redeem us from the debt of sin. We were like the man who owed his lord ten thousand talents, Matthew 18.24. We too have nothing to pay. God forgives us because **Christ** has paid it all.

Later on God punished David because he counted the people without collecting the half shekel of atonement money, 2 Samuel 24.2,10. Our Lord Jesus Christ never did any sin and so did not need to be redeemed. One day officers from the temple came to collect atonement money from Him. The Lord did not have to pay but He was ready to obey the law of God as other men did. He told Peter how he could get a coin to pay for the two of them. Read Matthew 17.24-27.

God began to tell Moses about the tabernacle in 25.1. We read there, *"The Lord said to Moses."* Now we are coming to the end of the rules about the tabernacle and we read these same words again six times: 30.11,17,22,34; 31.1,12. This fact shows that these instructions are just as important as the earlier ones.

The laver, 30.17-21.

Aaron and his sons were consecrated for their work by Moses at the command of God. The blood of animals was shed, sacrifices were burned and oil was put on the priests. Even before these things the new priests were washed with water at the door of the tabernacle, 29.4. Now God told Moses to make a laver of brass. The laver was shaped like a very large pot on a base, all made of brass. It was put at the door of the tabernacle so that the priests could wash their hands and their feet before they went inside. After going through the gate of the court the priest came first to the brass altar where a sacrifice was made for his sins. Then he washed his hands and feet at the laver before going into the presence of the Lord.

We do not know how big this laver was. Years later in Solomon's temple there was a "sea" which was 10 cubits or 15 ft. wide and 5 cubits or 7½ ft. high, 1 Kings 7.23. Solomon also made ten bases of brass which were used by the priests to wash their feet. The laver in the tabernacle was no doubt smaller than the sea in Solomon's temple. We have seen that the believer needs to keep himself clean every day by the water of the Word of God, Psalm 119.9.

The anointing oil, 30.22-33.

God told Moses exactly how to make the oil which was used to anoint Aaron, his sons and the tabernacle itself. This oil was not to be used for any other purpose whatever. If anyone made oil out of the same things, he would be cut off from the nation of Israel. The word *Christ* means the Anointed One. The Lord Jesus was *anointed* with the Holy Spirit, Matthew 3.16. From this we understand that oil speaks of the Holy Spirit.

It is a very serious thing to act as if you are filled with the Holy Spirit when it is not true. Paul did many wonderful things in the power of the Holy Spirit. When the sons of Sceva tried to do the same, they were put to shame. Read Acts 19.11-16. On the other hand God will not forgive men who speak against the

68

Holy Spirit and call His work the work of Satan, Matthew 12.24.32.

Incense for the gold altar, 30.34-38.

God also commanded Moses to make a special incense to burn on the gold altar. We have seen that the anointing oil was made of olive oil with four sweet smelling things mixed with it. For this incense also four sweet smelling things were mixed together. Again anyone who tried to make this for himself would be put out of the nation of Israel.

The Lord in these lessons is trying to teach us something about His holiness. When the men of Israel put up the tabernacle, it was in the center of the camp of Israel. Lepers and other people had to stay outside the camp, Leviticus 13.46. Any Israelite, man or woman, who was clean could enter into the court of the tabernacle and give his offering to the Lord. Only the priests, the sons of Aaron could go inside the tabernacle. Only the high priest could go into the Most Holy Place and then only once a year on the day of atonement, Leviticus 16; Hebrews 9.7.

As Christians we are called and commanded to enter into the presence of the Lord. Remember that it must always be with godly fear, Hebrews 12.28.

The workmen, chapter 31.

God gave Moses complete instructions for the material and the plan of the tabernacle and everything in it. He also told him the names of the two chief workmen.

The first and more important was Bezalel, the son of Uri, a son of Hur. As Hur was still alive, 17.10, Bezalel was still a young man at this time. His name means *"in the shadow of God"*. The Lord filled him with the Holy Spirit and gave him wisdom so that he could work cleverly with his hands.

His helper was Oholiab, of the tribe of Dan. The name Oholiab may mean *"the Father is my dwelling place"*. Moses himself wrote in the 90th psalm, *"Lord, thou hast been our dwelling place in all generations."* Many people think that Moses also wrote the 91st psalm. This speaks of the man who lives in the shadow of Almighty God.

Moses certainly learned the lesson of living in the presence of the Lord before trying to serve Him. Moses had to spend 40 years in the desert before leading Israel out of Egypt. The names of these two men who made the tabernacle make us think of these things. As we **live** in the presence of God we are made ready to **serve** Him. Even the Lord Jesus Christ spent a lot of time in prayer. He always stayed close to His Father's heart, John 1.18. Bezalel was called by name, v.2; filled with the Spirit, v.3; and given helpers, v.6. He was told to build the tabernacle and everything in it, just as the Lord had commanded Moses, v.11. God is still using young people who have learned to live with Him.

After giving all these instructions the Lord again told Moses to keep the sabbath day. This was a sign of His covenant with all generations of Israel, vs.12-17. Six days were given for work, but the seventh day was for the Lord. Anyone who did work on the seventh day must be put to death. This was a sign between Jehovah and Israel forever.

After all these words God gave Moses two large pieces of stone on which were written the ten commandments, v.18. Moses could show these tables of stone to the people of Israel and they would be sure that God had given them these ten commandments. We will see later what happened to these stones.

The sin of Israel, chapter 32.

In chapters 25-31 we have seen God's commands for building the tabernacle. In chapters 35-40 we shall read about the actual building of the tabernacle. Between the two, in chapters 32-34, we have the sad story of Israel's terrible sin.

Moses was in Mount Sinai with the Lord for 40 days and 40 nights at two different times, Exodus 24.18; 34.28. The first time Joshua went part way up the mountain and Moses met him on the way down, 24.13; 32.17. While Moses and Joshua were in the mountain, what was going on in the camp?

The people had promised to obey the commands of God, 19.8. After they received the ten commandments they promised again to obey, 24.3. Yet before Moses came down from the mountain, they broke the first and second commandments. They told Aaron to make gods for them, 32.1.

Waiting around with nothing to do is bad for anyone. To be idle for very long may lead to other sin, even the sin of worshipping idols. We also need to learn to wait patiently for God's time to come. The people did not **deny** that Moses had brought them out of Egypt, v.1. They should have believed that he would not leave them alone in the desert. He had been away from them for only a few weeks when they called on Aaron to make idols for them.

It seems that Aaron was with Moses in the mountain when God gave the ten commandments, 19.24. With the other elders he had seen the glory of God, 24.10. God had already commanded Moses to make Aaron the priest, 28.1. Aaron proved that he was completely unworthy of this honour. As soon as the people asked him he agreed to make gods for them. He told them to bring the gold ornaments which they wore in their ears. Jehovah had already said that the people could offer their gold to Him for the work of the tabernacle, 25.3. Later many of them did so, 35.22. Here they gave their gold for idols!

Christians also have to choose how they use their money: for themselves, or as a sacrifice to God. The love of money is a root of all evils, 1 Timothy 6.10. It is just as bad as worshipping idols, Ephesians 5.5, Colossians 3.5. On the other hand, if Christians give as a sacrifice, God is willing to accept their money. The Philippian Christians sent a lot of money to God's servant, the apostle Paul. This pleased God, Philippians 4.18.

The people brought their gold to Aaron and he melted it down. Then he took a tool and made the gold into the form of a young bull. In doing this Aaron did just what God had said not to do, 20.4. The people of Israel had worshipped idols when they lived in Egypt, Joshua 24.14, Ezekiel 20.18. Now they said that the gold bull had brought them out of Egypt. Aaron made Israel's sin still worse by building an altar before the idol. He also told the people that the next day would be a feast to Jehovah. God had already commanded Moses to keep His feasts on certain days, 23.14-17. Aaron had no authority to set aside another day for this purpose. The people brought their animal offerings. After eating and drinking they rose up to play or dance, v.6; 1 Corinthians 10.7. This playing or dancing means sin between men and women.

Men of God remembered this sin of Israel many years later, Nehemiah 9.18, Psalm 106.19. Jeroboam, a wicked king of Israel, followed the fathers' bad example, 1 Kings 12.28. Do you find it hard to believe that Aaron and the people of Israel would fall so quickly into such terrible sin? Remember that even born again Christians have the old sinful nature in them. If we stop following the Lord even for a short time we may fall into terrible sin.

Of course God in heaven knew what was going on in the earth,

71

vs.7-10. He told Moses to go down from the mountain because the people had fallen into sin. God told Moses that they had made a bull and were giving God's glory to the idol, v.8.

Moses was so surprised by these words that he could not speak. God went on to say that He would destroy Israel and make a great nation out of the children of **Moses**, vs.9,10. God in heaven had seen the **trouble** of Israel when they were in Egypt, 3.7. He came down to save them. Now He sees their sin. God had promised Abraham, Isaac and Jacob that He would make of their children a great nation. This promise could have been fulfilled through Moses, who was a son of Jacob. But God had also promised that the King would come through the tribe of Judah, Genesis 49.10. Moses was of the tribe of Levi. If God destroyed the rest of the people of Israel, His promise to Judah could not be fulfilled. God's words in verse 10 were to test Moses and do not mean that He might break His promise.

Moses' true love for the people of Israel is seen when he prayed to God for them. God called Israel the people whom **Moses** brought out of Egypt, v.7, but Moses called them the people that **God** had brought out, v.11. Moses told Jehovah that the Egyptians would be happy if He destroyed Israel, v.12. He asked the Lord to remember His promises to Abraham, Isaac and Israel, v.13.

It is a mark of the man of faith that he obeys God's commands at once. Moses usually did this, but here we see him doing what God did not tell him to do. God had said, "Let me alone", v.10, so that He could destroy Israel. Moses' prayer to God was also a mark of his faith. Moses knew the mind of God and after he had prayed God agreed to spare Israel, v.14. Of course God knew from the beginning what He would do and He was pleased to see Moses' faith.

We see other examples of this in the Bible. One day ten lepers came to the Lord Jesus. He told them to go and show themselves to the priest. As they went they were all cured. One of them was so happy about this that he went back to thank the Lord for curing him, Luke 17.11-16. Another example is Thomas. A week after the Lord had risen from the dead, He told Thomas to put his finger into His wounds and to put his hands into His side. Thomas did not obey this command. He was now quite ready to believe that Christ had risen from the dead. He did not need any more proof. He said "My Lord and my God", John 20.27,28.

It is interesting for us to think of these cases, but *we* should obey God's Word at *all* times. God has completely revealed His will to us. By His Word and by His Spirit He will show us what to do.

As Moses and Joshua came down from the mountain, they heard the noise which the people were making. Joshua thought it was the noise of war, but Moses understood that it was singing. When he saw them dancing around the gold bull he became very angry. He broke the tables of stone on which God had written the ten commandments. Moses felt the same way as God did about the sin of Israel. When he reached the camp he crushed the idol into powder, threw the gold dust on water and made Israel drink it as if they were drinking their own sin, vs.15-20.

When Moses called Aaron to give an account, Aaron tried to blame the people. He said that he threw their gold into the fire and the bull came out. If this were true, it would have been a great miracle which only God could have done. It would seem that Aaron tried tó put the blame on God for his own sin.

Adam did about the same when he fell into sin. He blamed his wife and called her *"the woman whom* thou *gavest to be with me,"* Genesis 3.12.

Moses broke the tables of stone because the people had already broken the covenant. Their promise to obey God's Law did not last very long.

Moses had punished the people and rebuked Aaron. Still many of the people were running around as if they had not fallen into a great sin, vs.25-29. Moses saw that some would have to die. The Lord commanded him to call for those who were willing to follow Jehovah. The men of Levi, Moses' own tribe, joined him at the gate of the camp. He commanded them to kill those who had rejected the word of God. The Levites obeyed the command of the Lord and this prepared them for their great work of caring for the tabernacle, Numbers 4.1-33.

God will never tell anyone today to kill a person, but in other ways we may find it hard to follow the Word of the Lord. If we obey God, He will prepare us for greater service for Him.

Moses went back to the Lord to pray for Israel, vs.30-34. He confessed that Israel had done great sin. He asked God to forgive them or else to take his own name out of God's book. God would not take Moses' name out of His book because of the sins of **others**. Instead He commanded Moses to lead the people into the land of promise. By this Moses knew that God would not destroy Israel.

73

Still He sent trouble or sickness on the people of Israel because of their sin, v.35.

Paul, like Moses, was ready to die for his people, Romans 9.3; 10.1. Moses and Paul praying for their own people make us think of the Lord Jesus Christ who is praying for God's children. If we fall into sin, God will not take away our eternal life, but He will surely punish us. When we sin, the Lord Jesus Christ prays for us. His prayer means that God can accept us even though we were sinful. Read again carefully Hebrews 7.25; 12.6, 1 John 2.1.

God is both holy and gracious, chapter 33.

God had to punish Israel for their sin. Because of Moses' prayer the Lord was able to keep Israel near Him and not destroy them. He promised again to do as He had said before to Abraham, Isaac and Jacob. Even if we do not believe, God remains faithful. He cannot deny Himself, 2 Timothy 2.13. Here God promised to send His Angel before them, but He Himself in His holiness would not go up with them. If God went with them, their sin would lead to God's judgment.

When the people heard this warning, they were very sorry, vs.4-6. They did not put on their ornaments and took off even the ornaments which they had on.

Before the tabernacle was built Moses went out to a tent when he spoke with Jehovah. This tent was just outside the camp. When Moses went out to worship, the pillar of cloud showed the people that Jehovah was speaking to Moses. The people in the camp watched all this, but Joshua wanted to stay in the tent before the Lord, vs.7-11. Jehovah talked to Moses as a man speaks to his friend.

The first half of chapter 33 teaches that a holy God must be separate from sinful people in the camp. Men of faith could go out of the camp to meet God. The rest of the chapter, vs.12-23, tells us Moses' words and God's words. Moses wanted three things, but really asked for two of them.

1. Moses wanted to know who would go with him as he led the people through the desert. He asked God to show him His ways, vs.12,13. God had warned Israel that He was holy and could not go among them, vs.3,5. In answer to Moses' prayer He agreed to go with him and them, v.14. God had told Moses that he had won God's favour, v.12. Moses said, "If this is so show me thy ways so that I may find more favour in your sight." In this chapter Jehovah

again called Israel "the people whom you have brought up out of Egypt." Moses asked Him to remember that the nation of Israel was His people, v.13. Moses was very happy to hear that God would go with them. He did not want to go anywhere alone without God, v.15. If the Lord went with Israel everyone would know the Israelites were His people, v.16.

The Lord Jesus does not ask us to go out alone and preach the Gospel and witness for Him. He does command us to go and teach all nations, but promises to be with us all the days, Matthews 28.19,20.

2. The Lord again promised to go with them, v.17. Moses then asked the Lord to show him His glory, vs.18,19. Perhaps Moses wanted to see something wonderful with his eyes. God told him He would show him the glory of His **character**. He would show Moses all His goodness and help him to know the name of Jehovah. God shows grace and mercy according to His own will. No one can demand that God should be gracious to him. God pours out free grace to those who have faith. There is nothing more wonderful than to know God and what He is like.

3. To know God's glorious character is much more important than to see anything with the eyes. Moses did not ask for anything else, but it seems that he wanted to see God's face. This however was not possible. No man can see God's face and live, v.20. Moses could not ask for this favour, so God kept on speaking. God told him that He would put him in a hole in the rock and cover him with His hand. When He had passed by Moses could see God's back, but not His face.

This rock makes us think of the rock which Moses struck so that water came out of it, 17.6. Both of these rocks speak of the Son of God, our Lord who was put to death for us. In the future we shall see God's face, Revelation 22.4. This is the face of the Lord Jesus Christ, the Son of God. Even now by faith "we see Jesus", Hebrews 2.9. We can see the glory of God in the face of Jesus Christ, 2 Corinthians 4.6. As we look to Him we will become more like Him, 2 Corinthians 3.18.

The covenant of Jehovah, chapter 34.

The covenant which God made with Israel through Moses on Mount Sinai is called the Sinaitic Covenant. It is called a **conditional** covenant because there was a condition: IF Israel obeyed God's Law, THEN God would bless them. In a conditional covenant God promises to do certain things if man does his part. God's covenant with Abraham was not conditional. God simply promised to give the land to the family of Abraham, Genesis 17.3-8.

Today God brings us into the covenant of grace. This covenant is unconditional. God has promised to save us from our sins. He can do this because the Lord Jesus has finished the work. God's promise does not depend on our good works.

The Sinaitic covenant, the covenant of Law, is conditional. God promised to bless Israel IF they obeyed His commands. Israel quickly promised to obey, but they did not know how weak they were. At first this covenant was given in the form of pure law, chapters 20-23. God commanded the people to obey and they promised to do so. When Moses went up the mountain again, 24.18, God gave him instructions for the tabernacle, the sacrifices and the priesthood. God knew that Israel would quickly break His commands. By means of the tabernacle, the sacrifices and the priesthood God could keep a weak and sinful people in the place of blessing near Him. An animal could die instead of the sinner. The high priest could pray for the people. The tabernacle made it possible for Israel to come near God. From all this we see that the second part of the covenant of law included grace.

In chapter 34 we learn that God is able to keep Israel in the place of blessing. They had broken the covenant in its first form, but in the second form the covenant had room for God's mercy. Moses had broken the two tables of stone. They stood for the first form of the covenant which was pure law, 32.19. Now God commanded Moses to cut two pieces of stone like the first and to come the next day to Mount Sinai, vs.1-4.

The top of Mount Sinai was 2200 ft. above the plain. Moses was in the mountain six times in all: alone, 19.20; with Aaron, 19.24; alone, 20.21; with Aaron and 72 others, 24.1; with Joshua for 40 days, 24.18; 32.17; and now alone, 34.3,28, this time also for 40 days.

This time the Lord met Moses again and announced His name as He had promised, 33.19. God had shown Himself to be a God of mercy and grace. He shows mercy to thousands of people and forgives their sin. He is also a God of truth and righteousness, who will punish men for their sins. When Moses heard these words, he worshipped the Lord. He asked God again to forgive Israel and to go with them, vs.5-9.

Moses also prayed that God would take Israel for His own. The Lord agreed to show more wonderful things to Israel than to any other nation, v.10. He would drive out other nations and give their land to Israel, v.11. Israel should not make a covenant with these nations nor follow their practices. They must obey the first command, vs.12-16. They should also keep the second command, v.17. Then the Lord gave again commands about the feasts, the firstborn, and the sabbath, vs.18-28. Read these verses carefully.

God wrote His commands on the tables of stone, v.1, and told Moses to write the words of the covenant, v.27. In 17.14 the Lord commanded Moses to write in a **book**. Moses also had the stories of the early fathers which we now call the book of Genesis. It is wonderful that God should keep these old books for us. We can know how He dealt with men in old times long ago. God still speaks to men through the Bible. It is His living active Word, Hebrews 4.12.

Moses came down from the mountain with a shining face, vs.29-35. He called Aaron and the elders together. At first the people of Israel were afraid because Moses' face was shining. When he came near he told them all the commands which the Lord had given to him. Moses put a veil over his face while he was talking to the people. He took it off again when he went into the tent to speak to Jehovah. He used this veil so the people could not see that the glory soon faded away, 2 Corinthians 3.13.

After Moses was in the presence of Jehovah, he showed God's glory for a short time. Our Lord Jesus Christ shows the glory of God fully and perfectly, Hebrews 1.3. As we talk with the Lord in prayer and hear His voice in the Word of God, some of His glory will be seen in us also. This is what happened to Peter and John. Even their enemies had to declare that Peter and John had been with Jesus, Acts 4.13.

Lesson 8
THE TABERNACLE WAS BUILT, chapters 35-40.

In chapters 25-31 God told Moses to build the tabernacle according to the plan. In chapters 35-40 we have the story of how they actually built it. First of all Moses gathered the people together to tell them the commands of the Lord, 35.1-3. The only command which he spoke of is about the sabbath of rest. No doubt Moses also told them the other commands which the Lord gave him in chapter 34. The sabbath was important. The people could not even light a fire on the sabbath. A man of Israel later gathered sticks for a fire and had to die for it, Numbers 15.32-36.

The offering, 35.4-35.

Then Moses told the people to bring their offerings to the Lord. They could bring metal, linen cloth, colouring material, skins of certain animals, oil, wood, sweet smelling powder and stones of great value, vs.4-9. All these things were to be used in making the tabernacle. Only people who were **willing** were asked to share in this offering.

Then Moses told the people what the offering was for. He gave a list of the different parts of the tabernacle and the furnishings, vs.10-19. The men who were wise and skilful could help in making the tabernacle.

Many of the people of Israel were very happy to give for this purpose. They were glad that God had forgiven their terrible sin and was willing to walk with them again. They gave gladly from their hearts, vs.20-24. The women could help, vs.25,26. The leaders gave what they could, vs.27,28.

Then Moses named Bezalel as the chief workman and Oholiab as his helper, vs.30-35. The Spirit of God gave them special skill to do this work.

In this chapter we read four times about the people giving from their hearts: verses 5,21,22,29. Five times we read of those who were able to prepare the materials, vs.10,25,26,31,35. Everyone of us is able to give something to the Lord and the Lord loves anyone who gives with joy, 2 Corinthians 9.7. We can each one also **do** something to build up the church of God. It is important to know what you are able to do and then to do it faithfully. The Holy Spirit makes us able to serve God, 1 Corinthians 12.7-12.

The work of the tabernacle, chapters 36-38.

God gave to Bezalel and Oholiab the skill they needed to make the furnishings of the tabernacle, 35.30-36.1. The people helped by making materials, 35.25; 36.8. Many others brought gifts which the workmen used. The people of God were thankful to the Lord and were glad to give Him the things which were theirs.

If Christian people today really loved their Saviour, they would give more for the work of the Lord. Some of the Israelites wanted to bring something to the Lord, but they waited too long. When there was enough of everything, Moses gave the command that the people should not bring any more, 36.6. Today is our time to serve the Lord, to live for Him and to give to His work. If we do, He will reward us in heaven. Our time to serve Him may not last much longer.

First the workers made the curtains of linen with their blue strings and gold wires or hooks, vs.8-19. They also made the coverings of goats' hair, and of the skins of sheep and goats. These were all made according to the command of the Lord in 26.1-14.

They made frames of wood and covered them with gold according to the command, vs.20-30. Here we learn that each frame had two "tenons" to hold the boards together, v.22. They also made bases of silver and rings of gold.

They made rods of wood covered with gold to hold the frames together, vs.31-34. Then they made the two curtains. One was to hang between the Holy Place and the Most Holy Place and the other hung at the front of the Holy Place, vs.35-38.

In chapter 37 we see that Bezalel made the box of the covenant, the table, the gold lamp, the altar of incense, the holy oil and the pure incense, v.29. In making these things he followed the commands which God had given to Moses. These four objects made of gold were used **inside** the tabernacle. We are not told again here how these things were to be used. The use of each object is found in 25.16,22,30,37; 30.7,30,36. We are told here that the two cherubim and the mercy seat were to be made out of **one** piece of gold, 37.7,8.

In chapter 38 Bezalel made the brass altar and the laver, vs.1-8. These two things were placed outside the tabernacle in the court. The laver was made out of brass mirrors which the women used to look at themselves.

We have seen that the laver speaks to us of the Word of God. The Bible is like a mirror which shows us our true nature, James

1.23,24. The Word of God is also like water which makes us clean, Ephesians 5.26. The Scriptures will also set us apart for God, John 17.17, and make us strong in the faith, Acts 20.32.

After this Bezalel and his helpers made the curtains for the court, then the pillars, bases and hooks. They also made the hanging for the gate of the court, vs.9-20.

The gold which was used in the tabernacle weighed nearly 30 talents, v.24, and would be worth about 2,000,000 dollars today. The people of Israel were quite willing to give their gold. The silver in the tabernacle weighed over 100 talents, vs.25-28. It would be worth about 175,000 dollars today. The people did not give the silver. They had to pay it as a tax, half a shekel for every man. A talent of silver was worth 3000 shekels. Some of the women gave the brass for the laver and other people gave brass for the bases. All the brass weighed over 70 talents.

You will see that the tabernacle was worth a great deal of money. The teaching about the tabernacle is precious to us because it all speaks of the glory of our Lord Jesus Christ. It is better to know the Lord than to have boxes full of money.

The clothes of the priests, chapter 39.

Bezalel and Oholiab made the clothes for the priests as the Lord had commanded Moses. They also made the ephod, vs.2-7; the breast piece, vs.8-21; the robe, vs.22-26; the linen coats, vs.27-29; and the turban for the priest's head, vs.30,31. These verses do not give us much more than what we have read before. It is good to know that the people of Israel did exactly what God had commanded.

We do learn that they beat the gold very thin and cut it into wires. These wires were worked in with the blue, purple, and scarlet in the fine white linen cloth of the ephod.

The gold speaks of our Lord Jesus Christ as the Son of God. When He was here in this world people did not see the full glory of God in Christ. In the ephod only a little gold would show with the blue, purple and scarlet. The Lord Jesus showed many different glories. Those who wanted to know Christ could get close enough to Him to see His glory as the Son of God as well. The four Gospels were written by four different men. Two of them, Matthew and John, were apostles and lived with the Lord for three years. In their books they showed the Lord as King, and as Son of God. The other two writers, Mark and Luke, may never have seen the Lord Jesus. The Holy Spirit led them to write books about the Lord as **Servant** and as the **Son of Man**. We see that the two men who were closer to Christ saw His glories in a higher way.

When the Lord told Moses about the ephod, He told him to set in it precious stones called Urim and Thummim, 28.30. We do not read of these again in chapter 39, but Moses put them in their place later on, Leviticus 8.8.

At last all the parts of the tabernacle and all the furniture were ready, vs.32-43. They brought these things to Moses and Moses saw that they had done everything as the Lord had commanded. Then Moses blessed the people who had worked on the tabernacle.

Ten times in this chapter we see that everything was made according to the plan: verses 1,5,7,21,26,29,31,32,42,43. This is quite different from the sin of Israel in later years when *"Every man did what was right in his own eyes,"* Judges 21.25. Today we ought to be careful to obey the commands of the Lord as given in, Scripture. If we do, the Lord Jesus will give us a blessing just as Moses blessed the people, v.43.

The tabernacle was set up, chapter 40.

Now everything was ready and God commanded Moses to set up the tabernacle and to put everything in its right place. Everything was to be anointed with oil because it was holy to the Lord. Aaron and his sons were to be washed, clothed, anointed, and set apart for God, vs.1-15.

Exactly one year after Israel left Egypt, 12.2, Moses built the tabernacle and put everything in its place. This was on the first day of the first month of the second year, vs.16-33. The cloud covered the tabernacle and the glory of the Lord filled it, vs.34-38. This cloud was a sign that everything had been done according to God's will. It showed that He was with His people in the camp of Israel. By the cloud He guided the people on their long journey. It is always a great joy for us to know that the Lord is with us and guiding us in His way.

THE TEACHING OF EXODUS

What can we learn about God and man in the book of Exodus?

God

There are a few wonderful words in the Bible which describe God's character. These words are called attributes of God. They help us to understand what God is like. One thing we can learn about God in Exodus is that He cannot be seen by the eye of man, He is **invisible**. Although the leaders of Israel "beheld God", 24.11, they did not see anything that would help them make an idol, Deuteronomy 4.15,16. The second command said that Israel was not to make an idol or an image, 20.4. *"No one has ever seen God; the only Son.....has made Him known,"* John 1.18. In Genesis the words "the Angel of Jehovah" are used of the Son of God. It was the Angel of Jehovah who spoke to Moses on Mount Sinai, Acts 7.37,38. All we know about God is seen in the Son of God.

In Exodus we see God doing many wonderful acts of power to help His people. He also sent judgment on wicked men. God's power to do anything is called His **omnipotence**.

God in heaven promised to be with Moses in Egypt, 3.12. He also promised to be with Israel in the wilderness, 33.14. God is **omnipresent**. This means that He can be anywhere and everywhere at the same time. The Lord Jesus has promised to be with all His disciples wherever they go preaching the Gospel in the world, Matthew 28.20.

God can know everything. He is **omniscient**. For example He knew Israel's trouble in Egypt, 3.9. God can know everything in the future. He knew that Israel would agree to obey the words of Moses. He knew that Pharaoh would not let Israel go until God showed His great power, 3.18,19. The high priest used the Urim and Thummim, "the lights and perfections" to learn the will of God who knows all things.

God is over all. He is **supreme**. He allowed the people of Israel to become slaves and then He delivered them. He wanted Israel to love Him and serve Him. God hardened Pharaoh's heart, 7.3; 9.12; 10.1.

Today we can be sure that God rules on the throne of heaven. He is in control of kings and nations. He works all things together for good for them who love Him, Romans 8.28.

Another wonderful truth about God is that He reveals Himself. All Scripture is a revelation of God and in Exodus we see Him revealing Himself to Moses, to Israel and to the Egyptians, 7.5. God is **light**. Those who refuse the light from God will get darkness instead. An example of this is seen in the ninth plague, 10.21-23.

God revealed Himself as the I AM, 3.14. He never changes. He revealed Himself as God Almighty to Abraham, Isaac and Jacob, but in Exodus His full character as Jehovah, the covenant God, is seen.

We learn the **righteousness** of God in the judgments which He poured on Pharaoh and the Egyptians. The Ten Commandments God gave to Israel teach His righteousness. The Law of God is perfectly fair. "Life for life, eye for eye, tooth for tooth, hand for hand, foot for foot," 21.23-25. God Himself would return on men any evil which they did to others, 22.22-24. In the ark we see the angels looking down on the mercy seat guarding the righteousness of God.

The book of Exodus also teaches God's **holiness**. At the place where God spoke to Moses the very ground became holy, 3.5. Moses could not continue on his journey as a servant of the Holy God until his son was circumcised, 4.24-26. When God came down to Mount Sinai, no man or animal could touch the mountain, 19.9, 10,13,21; 20.18, Hebrews 12.20. The whole tabernacle is a lesson on the holiness of God. The Israelite could bring a sacrifice to the altar of brass. The Levites could go further and serve in the court. The priests could enter the Holy Place. But only the high priest could enter the Most Holy Place, and then only once a year and only after offering sacrifices. From this Israel should learn that God is very holy. *So should we.*

The greatest attribute of God is His **grace**. God showed His grace richly to Israel, 34.6. God also showed grace to the Egyptians. When God sent the hail some of the Egyptians believed the word of the Lord and saved their cattle, 9.20. Some of them may have gone out with Israel as part of the *mixed group,* 12.38. In the Law God told His people how to treat any strangers who wanted to live with them, 12.49. Any Egyptian or any stranger who believed in Jehovah could share in God's grace to Israel.

Christ

Gold speaks of glory and therefore of the "God of glory", Acts 7.2. The gold in the tabernacle speaks of our Lord Jesus Christ as the *Son of God.* Gold was used in the ark, the lampstand, the altar of incense, the table, the veils, the hooks, the ephod, the frames and the poles.

Before the Son of God became a Man, His great work was to show men what God is like, John 1.18. He always revealed God's glory, Hebrews 1.3. Everything we know about God we learn through the Son. The Son revealed God many times in Exodus.

The Lord Jesus Christ was the *perfect Man*. The fine linen in the tabernacle and the clothes of the priests speak of Christ as a perfect Man. The acacia wood also speaks of Christ as a Man. The Son of God took on the nature of man, Hebrews 2.14. The wood was covered with gold and all you could see was gold. This teaches us that the more important thing about Christ is this: He is the Son of God. Bread without yeast makes us think of our Lord Jesus Christ because there was no evil thing in Him, John 18.38; 19.4; 2 Corinthians 5.21, 1 Peter 2.22. The servant who loved his wife and his master is a picture of Christ who became a Servant forever, 21.2-6.

The Passover lamb speaks in a wonderful way of Christ in His *death*. A perfect lamb was watched for four days. When the lamb was killed its blood on the door posts kept out the judgment of God. The meat of the lamb was put through the fire of judgment and then eaten by the believer. All the offerings speak of our Lord Jesus Christ. We will learn more about them in the book of Leviticus.

When a tree was cut down, it made the water sweet, 15.25. This speaks of the blessings which are the result of Christ's death. In the same way Moses struck the rock and the water poured out, 17.6. When the Lord Jesus died, eternal life came to all men.

The word apostle means *one who is sent*. Moses was sent by God and therefore is a picture of the Lord Jesus, Hebrews 3.1,2. At first the people of Israel refused to listen to Moses, 2.14, Acts 7.35. Years later Israel did the same to the Lord Jesus. God promised Israel that He would raise up a Prophet like Moses, Deuteronomy 18.15,18. This Prophet was the Lord Jesus, who spoke for God, Acts 3.22; 7.37. The Lord Jesus stands between man and God, 1 Timothy 2.5, just as Moses did, Exodus 20.19; 32.11-14. The Lord Jesus is our High Priest and Aaron is a picture of Christ in His service for us at this time.

As Christians we are travelling through this world, which is like a desert. God supplies all our needs in the Lord Jesus Christ, Philippians 4.19. So the manna speaks of Christ, John 6.30-35. The angel of Jehovah, the Son of God, kept Israel from the dangers of the way, 23.20. In giving us Christ God has given us everything, Romans 8.32, 1 Corinthians 3.21-23.

As the people of Israel traveled through the desert they looked ahead to the end of the journey. By faith they knew that they would enter the land of promise. Our hope is the coming of our Lord Jesus Christ. He will take us home to heaven to be with Himself.

The Holy Spirit

The cloud and the fire led the people of Israel through the desert. This is a picture of the Holy Spirit who leads us in the right way, Romans 8.14. The Lord Jesus was anointed as the Christ when the Holy Spirit came upon Him, Matthew 3.16. From this we see that the anointing oil in Exodus speaks of the Spirit of God, 29.7. We too have been anointed by the Holy One, 1 John 2.20,27. In Exodus we see that the Spirit of God was given to Bezalel so he could do the work of the tabernacle, 31.3; 35.31. To help the apostles build the Church the Holy Spirit filled Peter, Acts 4.8, Stephen, 7.55, Barnabas, 11.24, and Paul, 13.9.

Angels and Satan

We learn from the New Testament that angels delivered the Law, Acts 7.53, Galatians 3.19, Hebrews 2.2.

God created Satan as an angel, but he rebelled against God. Satan knew God's promise to raise up a Saviour from among the people of Israel. This Saviour would ruin all Satan's plans, Genesis 3.15, Hebrews 2.14,15. Satan put a wicked thought in Pharaoh's heart and Pharaoh commanded his people to destroy all the male children of Israel, 1.16,22. Satan is not all powerful like God, but he has greater power than any man. He gave power to the wise men of Egypt to copy the wonderful acts of God, 7.11,22; 8.7. Even then the wise men could only go so far, 8.19. These wise men were the false priests of Egypt and the judgment of God came on their gods also, 12.12.

Salvation

The whole story of the exodus is a picture of our salvation. Just as the Israelites were slaves in Egypt so all men are slaves of sin, John 8.34. God sent a saviour to lead Israel out of Egypt. The people were delivered by blood and by power. They believed Moses, their saviour, 4.31, but sometimes had doubts, 6.9. God led them into the desert where they had many problems and many enemies. All these things speak of the Christian's life in this world.

God gave Israel the Law *after* He had delivered them from slavery in Egypt. God did not plan to save anyone by the Law. We who are saved are not under Law, but under God's grace, Romans 6.14.

Believers who walk according to the Spirit fulfil the Law, Romans 8.4, but we are not saved by the Law. Even after God delivered them, the people of Israel often fell into sin, 14.11; 16.2; 17.2; 32.1-6. In the same way we believers still have the old nature and may sometimes fall into sin. The struggle with Amalek, 17.8-16, speaks of the long struggle between the old and the new natures, Ephesians 4.22-24.

On the other hand we also read of the sabbath of rest, Exodus 20.8-11. This speaks of the rest and peace which God has for us. God has done everything to save us. When we understand this truth we enter into His rest, Hebrews 4.4,10.

Prayer is another important part of the Christian life. In Exodus we read of the altar of incense which speaks of prayer. The priests could pray for other people. We should pray for one another. If we do not follow the Lord, we will fall into sin. Then the Father must punish us as He did the people of Israel, 32.20,28,35. We should learn these lessons of Exodus and keep from sin. If we do, the Father will not have to punish us.

The Church

The New Testament gives us the full teaching of the Church, but the Old Testament has a few pictures of the Church. The tabernacle is partly a picture of the Church as the place where God lives. The gold-covered frames speak of believers joined together by the Holy Spirit. The worship of the priests suggests the regular practice of believers when they meet together to worship God. We can praise the Lord for delivering us from slavery, as Israel did in chapter 15. We can bring gifts to God as Israel did, 35.21-29. The Church has in it both Jews and Gentiles, but most Christians were Gentiles. Moses took Zipporah, a Gentile, as his bride. In that way she was a picture of the Church, the Bride of Christ.

In many other ways the book of Exodus gives us pictures of New Testament truths. Every book in the Bible must be studied in the light of all other books in the Bible. As we come to know the whole truth of God we will grow in our understanding of God and His wonderful ways with men.

In order to understand God's Book and God's truth we must be willing to obey His commands, John 7.17. We must also be willing to spend a lot of time in studying the Bible. God the Holy Spirit will help us to understand the deep truth about God. Ask God to help you. When you learn a truth from the Bible tell others about it. This will also help you to understand it better.

THE BOOK OF LEVITICUS

LEVITICUS

The third book of the Bible was written by Moses. We learn this from the New Testament. The Lord Jesus told a leper to offer to Jehovah the things that *Moses* commanded, Mark 1.44. This command is found in Leviticus 14.10. Mary, the mother of the Lord, brought her offerings according to the Law of Moses, Luke 2.22-24, Leviticus 12.2-6. Paul in Romans 10.5 said that Moses had written Leviticus 18.5.

Most of Leviticus is an account of Jehovah's commands to Moses. God gave these commands after Israel had built the tabernacle, Exodus 40.17, Leviticus 1.1. Leviticus also tells us of events which took place in the first month of the second year after Israel had been delivered from Egypt. There are two important events in Leviticus. 1. Aaron and his sons were consecrated according to the command of God, chapters 8,9. 2. Nadab and Abihu, two of Aaron's four sons, turned from the command of the Lord and were destroyed, 10.1-5.

In Exodus we see that the tabernacle was set up. In Numbers we read of Israel travelling through the desert. Between these two, in Leviticus, Jehovah gave instructions for His people according to His own holiness. If the message of Leviticus could be put in one word, it would be **holiness**. The tabernacle was the way to enter the presence of God. Once a year the high priest as the leader of the nation could go into the Most Holy Place. Everything in the house of Jehovah is holy, Psalm 93.5. In Leviticus the most important chapters are those about the offerings, chapters 1-7, the day of atonement, chapter 16, and the Feasts of Jehovah, chapter 23. But every chapter has important lessons for us. Let us ask the Lord to show us these lessons.

Lesson 9

THE OFFERINGS OF JEHOVAH, chapters 1-7.

Hundreds of times we read that the Lord *spoke* to Moses. Four times it is written that the Lord *called* to Moses. Jehovah called to Moses out of the burning tree, Exodus 3.4. He called to him from Mount Sinai, Exodus 19.3,20. Now in Leviticus 1.1 He called him again. The tabernacle had been set up and the glory of the Lord filled it, Exodus 40.34. This time the Lord called Moses to give him commands about the sacrifices. In the Hebrew Bible the title of the third book is *"And He called."* These things show that the sacrifices were just as important as the commands given on Mount Sinai. Israel already had the tabernacle which they had made exactly according to the commands of Jehovah. Even with the tabernacle it was not possible for anyone to come near God without sacrifices. Both the tabernacle and the sacrifices speak of the Lord Jesus Christ in His different perfections.

There are five sacrifices in all and for four of them an animal was killed. The other one, the *"cereal"* or meal offering was made of flour. A man could bring a burnt offering, a meal offering or a peace offering whenever he wanted to. If anyone sinned he had to bring a sin or a burnt offering. The first three offerings are called *"offerings of a sweet smell"* to Jehovah, 1.9,13,17; 2.2,9; 3.5,16. The other two offerings were required by law and are not called offerings of a sweet smell. The meal offering speaks of the perfect life of our Lord Jesus Christ and the other four offerings speak of His death on the cross.

The Five Offerings

1.1-17	*Burnt offering*	animal	sweet smell
2.1-16	*Meal offering*	flour	sweet smell
3.1-17	*Peace offering*	animal	sweet smell
4.1-5.13	*Sin offering*	animal	required by law
5.14-6.7	*Guilt offering*	animal	required by law

The Burnt Offering, chapter 1.

God called Moses and started to tell him about the offerings, 1.2. A man could bring a bull or a sheep as an offering. If a man wanted to offer a bull for a burnt offering, it had to be a perfect animal, vs.3-9. The man should put his hand on the head of the animal. By doing this he was saying "This animal dies instead of me." The man then killed the bull and the priest put some of the blood on the brass altar. The man then cut off the skin of the dead

89

bull and cut the animal into pieces. When the fire was ready on the altar, the priests laid the parts of the animal in order on the wood. The legs and the inside parts of the animal were washed with water, and everything was burned as a sacrifice to the Lord.

If a man did not want to bring a bull, he could offer a male sheep or a male goat. The instructions were much the same, vs.10-13. If the person was very poor, he could bring a small bird, vs.14-17. In this case the priest killed the bird. He put the throat and the feathers of the bird with the ashes. He poured out the blood on the altar and burned the bird on the fire.

In the burnt offering the skin was kept for the priest, 7.8, but all the rest of the animal was burned on the altar. In the same way the Lord Jesus Christ gave Himself completely to God. He wanted only to do His Father's will, Psalm 40.7,8, Hebrews 10.7. When the Lord Jesus was in this world He did nothing but the will of His Father. He gave His life, His heart, His will completely to God. We can see this throughout the whole life of the Lord. Read with care Luke 2.49; 4.4,8, Matthew 17.5, John 18.11. The perfect life of the Lord Jesus made His death to be of great value. The sacrifice of Christ as a burnt offering was a sweet smelling sacrifice to God, Ephesians 5.2.

The burnt offering also speaks of the sacrifice of the believer. We ought to give our bodies to God as a living sacrifice, Romans 12.1, 1 Corinthians 6.20. Even our money when given to the Lord can be a sweet smelling sacrifice, Philippians 4.18. The Philippians gave so much to God that it made Him think of His Son who gave His all.

The Meal Offering, chapter 2.

The meal offering or the *cereal* offering could be a basket of fine flour with olive oil and frankincense. Frankincense was a kind of precious incense which comes from a tree. It was mixed with three powders to make the incense for the tabernacle, Exodus 30.34. In making a meal offering the priest took some flour in his hand and burned it on the altar. He also burned some of the oil and all of the frankincense. The rest of the meal offering was given to the priests, vs.1-3.

Instead of bringing a basket of flour the people could prepare it for eating. They could bring cakes of fine flour mixed with oil or with oil poured on top, vs.4-10. Again part of the offering was burned and the rest belonged to the priests.

No meal offering could have honey or yeast. Every offering had to have salt with it, vs.11-13.

While Israel was at Mount Sinai God gave commands about the *first fruits.* Later when Israel entered the land they were to obey these commands. If God gave them a good harvest they must bring some of the grain when it was first ripe, Exodus 23.19. A man could also bring an **offering** of his firstfruits. If he did he could bring yeast or honey with it, but this offering could not be burned on the altar, v.12. The offering must have oil and frankincense, vs. 14-16.

What does the meal offering speak of? In the fine flour there was no small stone or piece of dirt. It was pure and clean. The meal offering speaks of our Lord Jesus Christ as the Perfect Man. No evil at all was found in Him. Satan was allowed to put Christ to the test, Matthew 4.1. This test only proved that there was no sin in Christ.

God also allowed Satan to test Peter, Luke 22.31. As a result Peter fell into terrible sin, Luke 22.61. The only sinless Man is the Lord Jesus Himself.

In some cases the flour of the meal offering was put through the fire. The fire speaks of testing and troubles, 1 Peter 1.7. Every meal offering had oil which speaks of the Holy Spirit who came and remained on Christ, John 1.33. The frankincense speaks of the life of Christ bringing great pleasure to the Father.

The priest ate and enjoyed some of the flour and the oil, but all the frankincense was given to God on the altar. We as worshippers can understand *many* of the beauties of our Lord Jesus Christ as the perfect Man. Only God can understand *all* His perfections. The Lord Jesus always did what pleased the Father, John 8.29. He always spoke the Father's words, John 14.10. No wonder the Father was well pleased with Him, Matthew 12.18.

The Peace Offering, chapter 3.

The peace offering could be a male or a female of the herd, but it had to be perfect, vs.1-5. As with the burnt offering, the offerer put his hand on the head of the animal and then killed it. The priest put the blood on the altar. The fat and some of the inner parts of the animal were burned on the altar.

The rules are the same for a peace offering taken from the sheep, vs.6-11. In this case the fat part of the tail was burned as well.

In the same way an Israelite could bring a *goat* as a peace offering to the Lord, vs.12-17.

Part of the peace offering was burned but the offerer and the priests ate the rest of it as a holy meal before the Lord, 7.15,31,32. The peace offering speaks of the sacrifice of Christ bringing peace to men. God has always loved His creatures, but sin came in between God and men. God could not show His love toward men until He put away man's sins. In the cross of the Lord Jesus we see most perfectly both the love and the righteousness of God. Now we have *peace* with God, Romans 5.1,10. There is no longer a problem of sin between God and us. In the peace offering God received a part, and this was burned on the altar. The priest and the offerer also received a part, which they ate.

"God is satisfied with Jesus;
We are satisfied as well."

The Sin Offering, 4.1 - 5.13.

None of the five offerings in these chapters was for a person who sinned **and** knew at the time that he was sinning against the Lord. For example the man who broke the sabbath law was judged at once, Numbers 15.32-36. When David sinned he did not bring to God an animal for a sacrifice, Psalm 51.16. But if anyone broke the commands of the Lord **without** knowing it, he could bring a sin offering or a built offering, 5.14-6.7.

In chapter 4 we see that a *priest* might sin without knowing it. If he did, he was to bring a young bull, vs.1-12. If the whole *nation* sinned without knowing it, a bull must be offered, vs.13-21. If a *ruler* sinned, he could bring a smaller animal, a male goat, vs.22-26. If one of the *common people* sinned, he could bring a female goat, vs.27-31, or a female lamb, vs.32-36.

The person who had sinned must lay his hands on the head of the animal. If the whole nation was guilty, the elders laid their hands on the bull's head. The animal was then killed at the door of the tabernacle. If it was for a priest or for the whole nation, a little of the blood was dropped seven times before the veil. The priest put some of it on the horns of the gold altar and poured the rest at the bottom of the brass altar, vs.6,7,17,18. If it was for a ruler or for one of the common people, the priest put a little blood on the horns of the brass altar and poured out the rest at the bottom, vs. 25,30. The priest burned the fat and some of the inside parts of the animal as in the peace offering, vs.8-10,26,31,35. The skin and all the rest of the bull offered for the priest or the nation were burned in a clean place outside the camp, vs.12,21. The priest ate the sin offering of a ruler or a common person, 6.26,29. The priest made atonement for the nation, for a ruler or a common man. Then God forgave them, vs.20,26,31,36.

These verses have important lessons for us. One lesson is this: The cross of Christ does not mean that we are free to keep on sinning. God has forgiven the sins of the believer, but the Father will not let him go on in his sins. We also learn from this chapter that God expects more from those who know more. The priest should know more than the common people. If he sinned without knowing it, he had to bring a greater offering. God requires more from those who know the truth. Elders of churches, preachers and teachers are not free to do as they please. In fact they have to be more careful than others.

We have other cases in 5.1-6. A man might fail to tell what he knew, v.1. He might touch an unclean thing, vs.2,3, or break a vow without knowing it, v.4. In these cases he was guilty and had to bring a guilt offering, a lamb or a goat.

If he was poor, he could bring two birds, vs.7-10, one for a sin offering and one for a burnt offering.

If he was very poor, he could bring some flour without oil or frankincense, vs.11-13. These rules referred to both the guilt offering, vs.6,7, and the sin offering, vs.7,9,12.

The Guilt Offering, 5.14 - 6.7.

The guilt offering was also for a man who sinned without knowing it, but with the guilt offering he had to **pay back** as well. For example if a man failed to bring his tenth to the Lord he had to make it up and add a fifth part, 5.16. Suppose he received 100 pieces of silver. He should give ten to the Lord. If he only brought five at first, he had to bring the other five later. He also had to add one fifth, making six in all. Then he had to bring a ram for a guilt offering. The guilt offering was also used by a man who deceived his neighbour or robbed him in some way without knowing it, 6.1-7. He had to give back what he had taken and add a fifth part to it. Then he had to bring a ram to the Lord as a guilt offering.

These offerings teach us that God forgives sin only because Christ died for us. If a believer today falls into sin, we have One who stands for us before the Father. God forgives us because Jesus Christ, the righteous prays for us, 1 John 2.1,2. In the family of God the Father will not let His children sin without punishing them. If we confess He will forgive. If not, He will put

His hand on us, 1 Peter 5.6. The true born again Christian always wants to do his Father's will.

The laws of the offerings, 6.8 - 7.38.

General commands about the offerings to Jehovah are in the first few chapters of Leviticus. Now we have more rules for Aaron and the priests, 6.9. In this part of the book we have:

> the law of the burnt offering, 6.8-13;
> the law of the meal offering, 6.14-23;
> the law of the sin offering, 6.24-30;
> the law of the guilt offering, 7.1-10;
> the law of the peace offering, 7.11-18.

Dressed in his linen clothes the priest was told to gather the ashes of the **burnt** offering and put them beside the altar. Then he should put on other clothing and carry the ashes to a clean place outside the camp. The fire in the brass altar was to burn at all times day and night, vs.8-13.

Part of the **meal** offering, part of the oil and all of the frankincense was burned on the altar. Aaron, the priests and their sons should eat the rest of the meal offering, without yeast, in the court of the tabernacle, vs.14-18.

The priests also brought their own meal offerings every day, morning and evening. The priests' offering was burned on the altar and none of it was eaten, vs.19-23.

The priest was to eat the **sin** offering brought by a ruler or a common person. Other men and boys of the families of the priests could share in it, v.29. Only what was holy should touch the sacrifice. Anything else that came in touch with it became holy, and was to belong to Jehovah. If the blood fell on any piece of clothing, the owner had to wash it in a holy place. If they boiled the meat in a clay pot, they had to break the pot. If it was a brass pot, they had to clean it very carefully.

A priest could not eat a sin offering for a priest or for the whole nation. He had to burn it on the altar. In this case he dropped a little blood on the ground in the Holy Place, v.30; 4.5,6,17. So we see that the priest could eat part of some sacrifices, but he had to burn on the altar a meal offering or a sin offering made for the priest himself or for the nation.

In the law of the **guilt** offering, 7.1-10, we learn that some of the inside parts of the animal were to be burned as in the sin offering. The priest should eat the rest of it as in the sin offering. He also could have the skin of the burnt offering, v.8. A meal offering which was cooked belonged to the priest who offered it, but uncooked meal offerings were divided among all the sons of Aaron, vs.9,10.

The law of the **peace** offering shows that there were several kinds of peace offerings, vs.11-36. If the Lord answered a man's prayer and he wanted to give thanks to God, he could bring a peace offering. In this case he should also bring four different kinds of cakes of bread, vs.12,13. One of each kind was for the priest, v.14. The flesh of the sacrifice had to be eaten the same day, v.15. If a man brought his peace offering because he had made a vow, the flesh could be eaten the same day or the next day. If a man brought a peace offering of his own free will, they could eat the meat the same day or the next. Anything left after that had to be burned. If they ate anything on the third day, God would not accept the offering, vs.16-18.

If the flesh of a peace offering touched any unclean thing, they could not eat it, they had to burn it. The offerer could bring his family and other people to eat the peace offering with him, Deuteronomy 12.11,12. However only those who were clean could share in this holy meal. Verse 21 explains the word unclean, but we will learn more about this in chapters 12-15.

The Lord warned Moses again that the people should not eat fat or blood, vs.22-27. Anyone who did would be put out of the nation of Israel. The same thing would be done to anyone who ate part of the peace offering while unclean, vs.20,21.

The peace offering was divided into three parts: one for Jehovah, one for the priests, the rest for the offerer, vs.28-36. The offerer must himself bring the fat and the breast, v.30. The priest should burn the fat on the altar. This was the Lord's part. The breast belonged to all the priests. The upper part of the right leg was for the priest who made the offering, v.32. When God had received His part, He took care of His faithful servants as well. The last two verses tell again in short form what we have read in 6.8-7.36.

Many things about the sacrifices are hard to understand but we should look for pictures of the Lord Jesus Christ in His death. It is also interesting to think of the words of the Lord Jesus as found in the book of Psalms*. David in the Psalms often wrote of his own trials and problems, but the Holy Spirit led him to say things about the Lord Jesus Christ. For example in Psalm 40.8 we may hear the

* Another book, *EVERYONE HAS A PSALM*, will help you to understand better the teaching of the Psalms.

voice of the Lord Jesus giving Himself completely to God as in the **burnt** offering.

In Psalm 16.10 David spoke of someone who would not see the pit. Both Peter and Paul used this verse to show that the human body of the Lord Jesus did not decay even in the grave, Acts 2.27-31; 13.35-37. The **meal** offering of fine flour with no yeast in it makes us think of Christ, God's Holy One.

In Psalm 85.10 we see that righteousness and peace meet together. God the Righteous should put us away from Him forever, but He loves us and wants us to have perfect peace in His presence. Because the Lord Jesus died God can righteously bring us to Himself. We have peace with God and this is the lesson of the **peace** offering.

In Psalm 22.1 we hear the cry of the Saviour when He was at the lowest point of His time of suffering, Matthew 27.46. This was when God dealt with His Son because He had become the **sin** offering for us.

In the guilt offering the offerer gave back more than what he had taken away. On the cross the Lord Jesus paid the debts of others. He was without sin Himself, but paid it all for us. Psalm 69.4 makes us think of the **guilt** offering.

We will never be able to understand everything that the death of Christ means. The sacrifices of Jehovah in Leviticus 1-7 bring us many beautiful thoughts of Christ's sacrifice. As we remember the Lord's death for us, we should also remember **our** death with Him. If He was willing to give His all for us, we ought to be willing to give our all for Him.

Christ is the end of the Law and of the system of animal sacrifices, Romans 10.4, Hebrews 10.12,14. These animal sacrifices had to be made every day. This proves that they could not make the offerer perfect, Hebrews 10.1-4. The sacrifice of Christ was so perfect and complete that it never needs to be made again. The Lord has asked us to remember Him in His death by breaking bread and drinking the cup, not by making more animal sacrifices.

There are however three sacrifices which believers should make:

1. **Our bodies.** Instead of killing an animal we should offer our bodies as *living* sacrifices for His service. This means that I should use my hands and feet, eyes and tongue and ears, my body and mind, only for His glory, Romans 12.1.

2. **Praise.** When the Israelite wanted to praise or give thanks to the Lord, he could bring a peace offering, Leviticus 7.12. We

praise God with our lips, Hebrews 13.15. When we talk to others about Christ or give worship and praise to God, this is the sacrifice of praise.

3. **Money gifts.** The word *sacrifice* is used for giving what I need or want for myself. It is giving what really costs me something. Giving money to poor people or to the Lord for His work is a sacrifice to God. If I give so much that it is really a sacrifice, then God is well pleased with my gift, Hebrews 13.16.

God is pleased with my sacrifice because it makes Him think of His Son. The Lord Jesus Christ gave His all for us. God loves His Son so much that He likes us to make Him think of Christ. By living and giving sacrificially we can bring pleasure to the Father.

Abraham was willing to offer his only son to God, Genesis 22.2. Three brave men risked their lives to get some water from the well of Bethlehem to please David their lord, 1 Chronicles 11.17. David himself refused to give to God something which cost him nothing, 2 Samuel 24.24. The Lord Jesus praised a poor woman who gave all she had to God, Luke 21.1-4. *These are the sacrifices which please God.*

Lesson 10

PRIESTS AND PEOPLE, chapters 8-16.

We have read God's commands for the different sacrifices, chapters 1-7. Now God tells Moses how to consecrate the priests and the tabernacle, chapters 8,9. In this lesson we will also study the laws of unclean animals and people, chapters 11-15. After that there is the wonderful chapter on the Day of Atonement, chapter 16.

The consecration of the priests and the tabernacle, chapters 8,9.

First the Lord told Moses to take Aaron and his sons and gather all the people of Israel to the tabernacle, vs.1-4. When they came together Moses washed the priests with water. Then he put the priests' clothes on Aaron: the coat, the robe, the ephod, the breast piece and the turban on his head, vs.5-9. These things had all been made the way God had commanded, Exodus 28 and 39. Next Moses poured some oil on the tabernacle and everything that was in it. He poured some of the anointing oil on Aaron's head and put the priests' clothes on Aaron's sons, vs.10-13.

The first offering was the bull for a sin offering. Moses put some of the blood on the horns of the altar and poured out the rest at the bottom of the altar. He burned the fat of the bull and some of the inside parts on the altar. All the rest of the animal was burned outside the camp, vs.14-17. Then he killed the ram of the burnt offering and burned it as the Lord had commanded, 1.10-13; 8.18-21.

Aaron and his sons laid their hands on another ram, which was a special kind of a peace offering. Moses killed it and put some of the blood on the right ear, right hand and right foot of the priests. Then Moses took the fat, some of the inside parts of the animal and some of the bread. He put these into the hands of Aaron and his sons, also the upper part of the animal's right leg. Then these parts were burned on the altar. The breast of the animal belonged to Moses, vs.22-29.

After this Moses put some of the oil and some of the blood on the priests and on their clothes, v.30. Aaron and his sons boiled the rest of the meat and ate as much as they wanted, with the bread. Anything left over was burned in the fire. Aaron and his sons stayed in the tabernacle for seven days. They did everything just as the Lord had commanded Moses, vs.31-36.

At the end of the week the priests and the people brought more sacrifices, 9.1-7. First Aaron offered a young bull for a sin offering for himself, vs.8-11, then a ram for a burnt offering, vs.12-14.

When Aaron the high priest had been consecrated himself he was able to offer sacrifices for the people. The first was a goat for a sin offering, then a young cow and a lamb for burnt offerings, vs.3,15-17. He burned a little of the meal offering on the altar. Next he killed a bull and a ram as peace offerings for the people, vs.18-21. He burned on the altar the fat and some of the inside parts of each animal, but the breast and the upper right leg of each belonged to Aaron, 7.30-32.

Then Aaron lifted up his hands and blessed the people. Moses and Aaron went into the tabernacle, and the glory of the Lord appeared. Fire came from Jehovah and burned the offering on the altar, vs.22-24. This proved that God accepted the sacrifices of Israel.

What are the lessons in these services? Jehovah was teaching Israel that He is holy. Their priests could come near to God, but first animals had to die instead of the priests. By God's grace we can come near to Him, but He is still most holy. We must be careful to do everything according to God's Word. When Christians come together, they can enjoy worshipping in the very presence of God. It is therefore all the more important that they should come together according to the examples of the New Testament. It is equally important that they should walk every day in a holy way which will please the Lord. God's grace never allows us to walk according to this world or our own sinful desires.

Nadab and Abihu, chapter 10.

God had commanded Moses to set up the tabernacle, anoint the priests and offer the sacrifices. When everything had been done according to God's word, He showed His pleasure by sending fire to burn the sacrifices on the altar. This beautiful picture of blessing was soon spoiled by Nadab and Abihu. These men were Aaron's two older sons, Exodus 6.23. Acting in pride they thought they could bring their own burning incense to Jehovah. Once again fire came from the Lord, but this time to destroy the two priests, vs.1-3. Moses understood this to mean that men can come to God only in God's way and according to His Word.

Moses called two men of Aaron's family and told them to carry the dead men out of the camp, vs.4-7. Then he told Aaron and his other two sons that they should not be sad for the men who died.

99

The whole nation of Israel was to be sad for this sin and for the judgment of God on the guilty priests. Aaron and Eleazar and Ithamar should not go out of the tabernacle.

At this time Jehovah spoke to Aaron directly and not through Moses, vs.8-11. He told Aaron that the priests should not drink wine or strong drink when they went into the tabernacle. This suggests that Nadab and Abihu may have been drinking. God told the priests not to drink so they would not die, v.9, and so they would be able to know the difference between holy things and common things. They also were to teach the laws of God to the people of Israel, v.11.

Then Moses told Aaron and his sons to eat the rest of the meal offering and the peace offerings, vs.12-15. This would give strength to their bodies after this terrible event. It would also show them that God's plans for them had not changed.

At this time of trouble Moses also found that the goat for the sin offering had been burned. This goat was an offering for the people, 9.3,15. The blood had not been poured out in the holy place and the flesh should have been eaten by the priests, 6.26. Moses was angry with Eleazar and Ithamar, but Aaron had already noted this mistake. His sons had brought another sin offering and a burnt offering. Anyway the first sin offering should have been eaten before and now the time was past. When Moses heard these things he saw that nothing more could be done.

Our God is a destroying fire, Deuteronomy 4.24, Hebrews 12.29. His fire burned up the sacrifice of sinful men who repented, Leviticus 9.24. The same fire destroyed the men who rebelled, 10.1,2. At the beginning of a new age God plainly shows that His judgment is always according to His hatred of sin. The man who broke the sabbath law was judged at once, Numbers 15.32-36. In the New Testament Ananias and Sapphira lied to the Holy Spirit and were judged at once, Acts 5.1-11. No doubt many other men have done these things or worse. It might seem today that God does not judge sinners. We can be sure that God's time will come to judge all men righteously.

This chapter again teaches that God requires perfect holiness in those who come to Him. Nadab and Abihu had seen the glory of God, Exodus 24.1. God judged them for trying to come to Him according to their own ideas. As believer-priests our sins have been washed in the blood of the Lamb. We should walk every day in a holy way according to God's Word. Men should lift up *"holy hands"* when they pray, 1 Timothy 2.8. We should not try to come to God according to human plans or man's wisdom. We should draw near to God according to His Word, Hebrews 10.22. Holiness is right for God's house forever, Psalm 93.5.

LAWS ABOUT UNCLEANNESS, chapters 11-15.

God wanted His people to keep themselves clean. In this part of Leviticus He gave commands to Moses and Aaron about unclean food, chapter 11; uncleanness after a baby was born, chapter 12; unclean lepers, chapters 13,14; and uncleanness after something has flowed from the body, chapter 15. An unclean person could not share in the service of Jehovah, 7.19-21, Numbers 9.6,7.

Clean food, chapter 11.

Here the Lord tells the people of Israel what they could eat and what they could not eat. Two things are said about **clean** animals: the way they eat and the way they walk, vs.1-8. Some animals might seem to be clean according to one rule, but not the other. The names of four unclean animals are given in these verses. The people of Israel usually ate the meat of the bull, the sheep or the goat. God told them not to eat the flesh of an unclean animal nor touch its body after it had died.

In the first ten chapters of Leviticus we have read many laws about the worship of Israel. God demanded holiness in their worship. In chapter 11 we see that God also demanded holiness in the daily life of His people. We as Christians need this lesson as well. We do not have in the New Testament laws about what we should eat. The Lord Jesus taught that the heart is more important than the body, Matthew 15.1-20. We should not feed our minds with unclean things. It is important to read and see and listen to good clean things. In *"chewing the cud"* the animal brings back into its mouth the food which it has eaten. For the believer this seems to suggest that we should quietly go over the truths which we have partly learned from Scripture. This is the only way to know deeper things about God.

At the same time it is important that we **walk** as God has commanded. Isaiah the prophet was greatly used as a servant of God. He woke up early in the morning to think about God's Word. He also walked separately from this world. The more he walked with God the more people hated him, Isaiah 50.4-6. Jeremiah also thought carefully about the Word of God. *"Thy words were found and I ate them and thy words became to me a*

101

joy and the delight of my heart," Jeremiah 15.16. He too walked separately from the world and in fellowship with God.

The people of Israel could eat certain kinds of fish, vs.9-12. They could eat some birds, but the Lord gave a list of 20 birds which they could not eat, vs.13-19. The people of Israel could not eat most of the little things that fly and walk along the ground. The Lord gave the names of four which they *could* eat, vs.20-23.

Anyone who touched the dead body of an unclean animal would be unclean for the rest of that day, vs.24-28,39,40.

The names of eight other small animals are given, all unclean, vs.29,30. The dead body of any unclean animal might fall on some clean thing. If it did, the clean thing would become unclean. Anything made of wood, a piece of clothing, a pot or any food in the pot or any seed, all became unclean. The owner could wash some of these things and then they would be clean again. Others should be broken and thrown away, vs.31-38.

God also called unclean all little creatures that come over the earth in great numbers, all little creatures with many feet. The people of God should not make themselves unclean with these things. God is holy and His people should be holy, vs.41-45.

Why did God give these commands? One reason is the **health** of the people. For example the flesh of a pig can make people sick if it is not well cooked, v.7. Many other little creatures that fly or run along the earth can spread sickness. The great lesson of this chapter however is that we should be holy. We should not feed our minds on unclean things. The most important book to read is the Bible. When we read other books, we may be wasting time, and some books and pictures are very bad for a Christian. On the other hand the Bible is a treasure-house of truth, full of precious thoughts about God and about Christ. You could study the Bible and think about it all the days of your life and still not know everything about it. *"Whatever is pure, whatever is lovely....think about these things,"* Philippians 4.8.

Women after having a baby, chapter 12.

After a little boy was born in Israel the mother was "unclean" for seven days. The word unclean means that she had to keep away from holy things, vs.1-5. It is no sin for a woman living with her husband to have a baby. She was unclean for seven days the same as she was at the time of her monthly sickness. On the eighth day the baby boy was circumcised. The mother continued unclean for 33 days more. She could not come into the court-yard of the tabernacle or touch any holy thing. If it was a little girl the mother was to be separate for 80 days.

At the end of 40 or 80 days she was to bring a lamb for a burnt offering and a bird for a sin offering. If she was too poor to bring a lamb, she could bring two birds, vs.6-8. Mary the mother of the Lord Jesus brought the offering of a poor person when her first Son was born, Luke 2.21-24.

Here again God had good reasons for giving these commands. One reason was the health of women. There is also a spiritual meaning. It is plain that all men are weak and helpless when they are born. They are also unable to help themselves when they die. *"We brought nothing into the world and we cannot take anything out of the world,"* 1 Timothy 6.7. These chapters in Leviticus teach us that man is also **unclean** when he is born and when he dies. The mother is unclean for a few days after her baby is born. Anyone who touched a dead body was unclean for seven days, Numbers 19.11. When the father circumcised his baby boy he cut off the flesh and the boy became a member of the nation of Israel. When sacrifices were offered the mother became clean and could again come into the courtyard of the tabernacle.

How to tell if a man is a leper, chapter 13.

Leprosy is a sickness, not a sin. If anyone touches a leper, he may get leprosy also. A man who was a leper had to live outside the camp of Israel until he was cured.

Chapter 13 showed the priest how to tell if a man was really a leper. Many different signs of leprosy are given in verses 1-44. For example, a spot or rising in the skin or a white hair. If the priest was not sure he could shut the man up by himself for seven days. If the leprosy had spread in the man's body, the priest would know that he was a leper.

It is very important that the priest should know for sure if the man was a leper. If the priest found that he was unclean, the leper had to tear his clothes and cover his upper lip with a cloth. He had to cry, *"Unclean, unclean"*, and live outside the camp, vs.45,46. This was so he would not come near other people and pass on the disease to them. The leper could not live with his family nor bring a sacrifice to Jehovah. He had to warn people not to come near him.

The word leprosy is used in this chapter for diseases of the skin and diseases in clothing which might spread to other people. A man might bring a piece of clothing to the priest if he thought there was any disease in it. If the disease did not spread after seven days, the clothing should be washed. After another seven days the priest would look at it again and decide whether it was clean or unclean. If the priest decided that a piece of clothing was unclean because of a disease in it, the clothing must be burned, vs.47-58.

Cleansing of the leper, chapter 14.

When the leper was healed, he could bring sacrifices and live in the camp once more. On the first day he took two live clean birds, some wood, some scarlet colour and a plant called hyssop. The priest killed one bird and put the other bird quickly into the blood of the first and took it out again. He did the same thing with the wood, scarlet and hyssop. Then the priest put a little blood seven times on the leper who was healed and told the leper that he was clean. The priest let the living bird fly away. The cleansed leper had to wash his clothes, cut off all his hair and wash his body. He could then come into the camp, but could not live in his own tent for another seven days, vs.1-9.

When the week had passed, the cleansed leper brought a male lamb for a guilt offering, another for a sin offering and a female lamb for a burnt offering, vs.12,19,20. He also brought flour for a meal offering. The priest put a little of the blood of the guilt offering on the right ear, hand and foot of the leper, v.14. The leper also had to bring some oil. The priest dropped some of this from his finger seven times before Jehovah. Then he put a little oil on top of the blood on the right ear, hand and foot of the cleansed leper. The rest of the oil in the priest's hands was put on the head of the leper.

Moses put a little blood on Aaron's right ear, hand and foot, 8.23. The blood speaks of the sacrifice of Christ. For the cleansed leper, the oil on top of the blood speaks of the Holy Spirit. In this way the cleansed leper was set apart for Jehovah. He should listen to the word of the Lord (with his ears); he should do the Lord's will (with his hands), and go where the Lord wanted him to go (with his feet).

If the leper was poor he could bring a lamb for a guilt offering and two birds for the sin and burnt offerings, as well as the meal offering, vs.21-32. The blood and the oil were put on the cleansed leper as in the first case.

A leprous disease might appear in a house as well as in clothing, vs.33-55. Before the priest came to look at the house the owner should take everything out of it. If the priest found after seven days that the disease had spread, the owner could take out some of the stones and put in others. If the disease still spread after that, they had to break down the whole house and carry everything away to an unclean place. Everyone who came into the house while it was still standing became unclean.

If the priest found that the disease was gone, he would say that the house was clean. The owner could bring sacrifices as in the case of a leper who was cleansed.

Leprosy in Scripture speaks of sin as making man unclean in the sight of God. Leprosy spreads from one person to another; so does sin. Anyone who sins is by his example teaching others to do the same thing. We must not allow sin to continue in the church. A leper had to be put out of the camp. A wicked person must be put out of the church, 1 Corinthians 5.13.

Before anyone is put out of the church, it must be quite clear that he is guilty. The priest had to watch the leper for a number of days before saying that he was unclean. If you hear that someone has fallen into sin, you should first go to him alone, Matthew 18.15-18. If he will not listen to you, you should go again with one or two others. Only spiritual men can be of help in these cases, Galatians 6.1. If the person still will not listen, then the church must act. The church of God must be holy just as the camp of Israel had to be holy. This will mean that the sinful person must be put out of the church. However when he repents, he should be brought back again. In 1 Corinthians 5 we read of a man who had to be put out of the church. In 2 Corinthians 2 Paul wrote that he should be brought back again.

Unless sin is quickly judged, it will spread through the church. This is true of false teaching also. The church cannot receive anyone who comes with a new doctrine, 2 John 9-11. Any kind of sin brings sorrow to the Lord, Revelation 2.14,20. The church must keep itself pure.

Discharges from the body, chapter 15.

Only a few people become lepers, but all men and women have discharges when something flows from the body. These discharges made the man or woman unclean. The unclean person made others unclean, also the bed, clothing, or anything he might sit on.

If it was the usual natural discharge from the body, a man was unclean for one day. If it continued in an unnatural way, he was unclean for a week. A woman was unclean at the time of her regular discharge for seven days. If it continued for many days she would be unclean all that time and seven days more. When a man or woman became clean, he or she must bring two birds for a sin offering and a burnt offering, vs.14,15,29,30.

This chapter teaches us that we have sin in our inner nature. When this evil comes out others are made unclean. Only the cross of Christ can make us clean and only the power of Christ can keep us clean.

The Day of Atonement, chapter 16.

We have seen that God punished Aaron's two older sons by putting them to death. They tried to come into God's presence in the wrong way. In chapter 16 the Lord told Moses the *right* way for Aaron to come before Him and enter the Most Holy Place.

First Aaron had to bring a sin offering and a burnt offering for himself and his family. He was to take off his beautiful priestly clothes, wash himself, and put on his linen clothing with the linen turban. He should also bring two goats for the nation of Israel, vs.1-5.

After making his own offering Aaron was to draw lots on the two goats. One of the goats was offered as a sin offering and the other one was let go alive in the desert, vs.6-10.

Drawing lots was an Old Testament way of finding out the Lord's will, Joshua 18.6,10, 1 Chronicles 25.8, Nehemiah 10.34. The apostles drew lots when they wanted to know God's will, Acts 1.26. Now the Holy Spirit has come and we have the complete Bible. We can find out God's will by prayer and by studying His Word.

Aaron took a gold pot full of burning coals. With his hands full of sweet incense he entered into the Most Holy Place. There he put the incense on the fire and a cloud of smoke filled the place. Then Aaron put some of the blood of the bull on the front of the mercy seat and on the ground before the mercy seat, vs.11-14.

When he went outside he killed the sin offering for the **people**, vs.15-19. He took some of the goat's blood and went in again to the Most Holy Place. No one could be inside the tabernacle when Aaron did these things. When he came out again, he put some of the blood of the bull and of the goat on the horns of the brass altar. He also dropped a little blood on the altar seven times.

When Aaron had done all these things, he was to take the live goat, vs.10,20-22. He put his hands on the head of the goat and confessed the sins of the nation of Israel. Then someone led the goat into the desert and let it run away. Azazel is not the name of a devil. God told His people not to make sacrifices to devils, 17.7. One goat died for the sins of the people. The other carried their sins far away. The two goats make a wonderful picture of how God puts away our sins.

The prophet Micah knew that God would throw all Israel's sins into the deep sea, Micah 7.19. God not only forgives our sins, He forgets them also, Jeremiah 31.34, Hebrews 8.12. This is possible because the Lord Jesus Christ has paid the full price for our sins. God does not want us to keep thinking or talking about past sins. If we confess our sins to God, we should believe that He has forgiven us and be glad, 1 John 1.9. Then we should go on and try to do greater things for Him.

After this Aaron entered the tabernacle again and took off his linen clothes, vs.23-28. He washed his body with water and put on his regular beautiful clothing, Exodus 28.2. Then he went outside again and offered two sheep for burnt offerings, for himself and for the people. He also burned the fat of the sin offering on the altar. Someone burned the rest of the sin offerings outside the camp. The man who led the live goat into the desert had to wash himself and his clothes before coming back into the camp. The man who burned the sin offerings had to do the same.

God gave all the commands in the book of Leviticus in the first month of the second year. This chapter tells about the day of atonement which did not come until the tenth day of the *seventh* month. God told Israel to keep the day of atonement every year. After Aaron had died, one of his sons would be anointed to take his place. The son would make atonement for the tabernacle, the altar, the priests and all the people, vs.29-34.

The word *atonement* is found in this chapter 15 times and the word *atoning* once. The word *atonement* in the Old Testament means *covering*. On the day of atonement the sins of Israel were *"covered"* for another year. In chapter 16 we read seven times that this atonement was for all sins, vs.16,21 (three times), 22,30,34. This atonement was for all the people, vs.17,33. However even in Leviticus we learn that these sacrifices were not perfect. Men would be cut off from Israel for committing certain sins, for example 17.4,10; 18.29; 20.2,3. More, the sacrifices of the day of atonement were of value only for one year. Also these sacrifices covered the sins of the nation for a time, but they did not give the people of Israel victory over sin.

In the New Testament God has given us a far better way:

1. The blood of a Perfect Sacrifice has been shed, Hebrews 9.14.

2. This one Offering is of value forever, Hebrews 9.25-28; 10.11-14. Sins are not just *covered* for a short time. God forgives them forever.

3. Still more, the believer is *justified,* Romans 5.1,9. This means that God has put us in a different position before Him. He will never judge us as guilty sinners.

4. In Christ we have power to gain victory over sin, Jude 24.

5. Under the Law only the high priest could enter into the Holiest, and then only once a year. Now **all** the people of God at **any** time can enter into the Holiest with the blood of Jesus, Hebrews 10.19-22.

WHAT A WONDERFUL SAVIOUR!

Lesson 11
LAWS AND FEASTS, chapters 17-23.

In Exodus 20 we noted the ten commands which God gave to Moses. In Exodus 21-23 are the judgments of Jehovah. These are laws which explain the ten commands. The rest of Exodus and the first part of Leviticus tell of the tabernacle, the priesthood and the sacrifices. Now in Leviticus 17-22 we have more laws for the people. They could come to God by tabernacle, priest and sacrifice. They must also walk and act as God commanded.

First of all the Lord commanded that the people of Israel must bring their sacrifices to the tabernacle, 17.1-9. They could not kill an animal anywhere except at the door of the tabernacle. There the Lord received His part which was the fat burned on the altar. The priest also received a part of the peace offering. The man and his family could eat the rest of it. God did not want them to offer sacrifices to devils or spirits, v.7. Anyone who broke this law would be cut off from the nation of Israel, vs.8,9, 1 Corinthians 10.20.

The next command is against eating blood, 17.10-16. Long before this God had told Noah that he should not eat meat with the blood in it, Genesis 9.4. *"The life of the flesh is in the blood."* Still more important, the blood was used for making atonement, v.11. If anyone went hunting and killed an animal or bird, he must pour out the blood and cover it with dust.

Again the Lord said that the life was in the blood and anyone who ate blood would be cut off. When an animal died or was killed by wild animals, most of the blood would still be in the body. God's will was that His holy people should not eat such meat, Exodus 22.31, Deuteronomy 14.21. If anyone did eat this meat, he must wash himself and his clothes and be unclean all that day.

The early Christians thought it was important not to eat blood. The church at Jerusalem sent a letter to Gentile Christians telling them it was not necessary to keep the law of Moses to be saved. They did ask that the Gentiles would keep themselves from four things: (1) meat which had been offered to idols; (2) blood; (3) the meat of animals from which the blood had not been poured, and (4) adultery, Acts 15.23-29. Other New Testament verses teach us very plainly God's will about adultery, 1 Corinthians 6.18, and meat which had been offered to idols, 1 Corinthians 8.4-13. We read nothing more in the New Testament about eating blood, but the command given to Noah should be enough for those who are trying to please God.

All these commands came from Jehovah, the God of Israel, 18.1-5. The people had come out of the land of Egypt and were going to Canaan. God told them not to follow the sinful habits of the people of Egypt or the people of Canaan. They must obey God's commands and people who obeyed would live.

To obey and live is not the same as getting eternal life by faith in the Lord Jesus. A man would live IF he could keep the entire law of God perfectly from the time he was very young. But we are all sinners and we can get eternal life only by faith, Galatians 3.10-12.

God told His people not to marry a near relative, 18.6-18. A man must not marry his mother or his father's wife. He must not marry his sister nor the daughter of his own son or daughter; nor the sister of his father or mother. He could not marry his brother's wife nor the daughter or sister of his own wife.

We know today that people who marry a near relative may have unhealthy children. As believers we should try to do those things that please the Lord. In the New Testament God tells us very clearly not to marry an unbeliever, 2 Corinthians 6.14,15.

Other terrible sins are listed in verses 19-23. Sin between man and woman, between man and man, Romans 1.27, or between man and animal may be common today. Still they are sin in God's sight. Molech, v.21, was a god of the Ammonites, 1 Kings 11.7. God told Israel not to follow Molech, but sometimes they did, Acts 7.43.

The people of Israel should not make themselves unclean by following the evil habits of the nations in Canaan, 18.24-30. God was going to put these people out of their land and give it to Israel. Already their sins were so bad that the land itself was ready to throw them up, v.25. If Israel followed their sinful example, the same judgment would come on them.

In chapter 19 God again gave several commands which we have seen before. He also added some new ones.

The people should be holy like God. They should honour mother and father and keep God's day of rest. They should not worship idols, 19.1-4.

The Lord told them again about the peace offerings, vs.5-8. He told them to be kind to the poor, vs.9,10. They should not steal or lie, vs.11,12. A man should be fair to his neighbour and his servant. He should not be unkind to those who cannot hear or see, vs.13, 14. The people of God should be fair in judging others, vs.15,16, and love their neighbours, vs.17,18.

The teaching of many of these verses can be put in these words, *"You shall love your neighbour as yourself. I am the Lord."* v. 18. The Lord Jesus Himself agreed that the whole Law can be put in these words, *"You shall love the Lord your God, and your neighbour as yourself."* If you ask *Who is my neighbour?"* the Lord gave the answer to that question also. He said you should love anyone who needs your help, Luke 10:25-37. The best way we can help people is to give them the Gospel.

The people of Israel were not to mix things in an unnatural way, v.19. From this we can learn not to mix the things of God and the things of this world. We cannot serve two masters, Matthew 6.24.

Special laws for the case of sin with a slave girl are in 19.20-22. The fruit of the trees was holy to the Lord, vs.23-25. People should not eat flesh with blood in it nor listen to evil spirits, vs.26,31, nor follow the habits of the nations, vs.27,28. No man should let his daughter go into a life of sin for pay, v.29. All should keep God's sabbath, v.30. All should honour older people, v.32, and be fair to strangers, vs.33,34. They should be fair and righteous in buying and selling, vs.35-37.

We see that God's commands come down to our common life of every day. Anyone who says he is a Christian should act like one at all times.

The short command about Molech, 18.21, is found again in a fuller way in 20.1-5. A man who gave his children to Molech was to be stoned to death. If the people of Israel did not punish this man, God Himself would cut him off.

Again the Lord told His people not to listen to wicked spirits, v.6. Anyone who did must be stoned by the people, v.27. Anyone who cursed father or mother should be put to death, v.9.

Sin between man and woman, man and man, or man and animal is very wicked in the sight of God. We can see this because the commands of chapter 18 are given again in 20.10-21. If God says anything once, everyone should obey. If He says it twice it is still more important.

Israel was to be a holy nation to the Lord. God was about to bring them into a wonderful land. They must not follow the habits of the people of the land but must be holy for Jehovah, 20.22-26.

We should be perfect like our heavenly Father, Matthew 5.48.
We should be holy as God is holy, 1 Peter 1.16.

111

The people of Israel had to be holy, and the priests still more so. The priests had special rights and God expected more of them. We read of some of the special laws for the priests in chapter 21 and some of their special rights in chapter 22.

For example the priest could not make himself unclean by burying a dead person unless it was a close relative, 21.1-9. The command for the priests, about cutting the hair on face or head, 21.5, is a little different from the rules for other men, 19.27. A priest had to be very careful about getting married, v.7, and also about his daughters, v.9.

The high priest had to follow still stronger rules, 21.10-15. He could not bury even his own father or mother. He could not marry a woman who had been married before.

Only the sons of Aaron could serve as priests, and only those of his sons who had perfect bodies. Anyone who could not see or walk well, anyone who could not stand up straight could not serve as priest. However he could eat food with the other priests, 21.16-24.

Today all God's people are priests. We must live according to God's highest laws. Both sacrifices and priests were pictures of our Lord Jesus and both had to be perfect, Exodus 12.5.

The priests also had special rights. They served the Lord in the tabernacle. For their food they had part of every sacrifice except the burnt offering. However a priest who was unclean for any reason could not eat the holy food, 22.1-9.

The priest's family also ate this food, but a visitor or a servant or a married daughter could not eat it, 22.10-16. If anyone ate some of the holy food by mistake, he had to pay it back and add a fifth part to it.

It was the duty of the priests to accept only perfect offerings from the people of Israel, 22.17-25. These sacrifices were pictures of the Lord Jesus Christ. For a free will offering an animal with some part too long or too short could be accepted, v.23. If it was a *"votive"* offering, given to keep a vow, it had to be perfect. This does not teach that Christ is less than perfect, but that our **understanding** of Him may be less than perfect.

A young animal had to be at least eight days old before it could be offered as a sacrifice, 22.26-30. Even then the people could not kill the mother and the young one on the same day. All these commands were given by Jehovah, the Holy One. He saved Israel from the land of Egypt and had a right to tell them what to do,

22.31-33.

Some of these laws teach us that God is holy and Christ is perfect. Other laws were given to keep Israel from following the evil habits of the people who lived around them. Some were for their own good. Others showed that God loves my neighbour as well as me. Some of these laws are hard for us to understand today. The rules concerning the sacrifices, the priesthood and the tabernacle are called *"ceremonial laws"*. All these have been done away in Christ, Romans 10.4. We have no blood sacrifice, special priesthood or holy tabernacle today. Other laws which tell us how to act toward other people may be called *"moral laws"*.

We as Christians should certainly obey God's moral laws, but not as a means of salvation. We are saved not because we keep the Law, but because Christ paid the debt for our sins. When we are born again we keep the laws of God because we love Him, because the Holy Spirit lives in us, Romans 8.4.

The Feasts of Jehovah, chapter 23.

In Leviticus 23 we read first about the sabbath which was to be kept every week. After that we have the seven feasts of Jehovah which were to be kept once a year.

God gave Israel commands about the sabbath when they first left the land of Egypt, Exodus 16.5. In Egypt they were slaves and had to work every day without pay and without any day of rest. When Israel walked in the desert God gave them food for the sabbath day so they did not have to go out to gather the manna, Exodus 16.25,26. God gave Israel ten commands; the fourth one was about resting on the sabbath day, Exodus 20.8-11. This command was given again in Deuteronomy 5.12-15.

In verses 1-3 of our chapter God commanded the people to work six days and to rest one day. Many years before He had put a curse on the ground because of Adam's sin. From then on Adam and all his children had to work for their food day by day, Genesis 3.17-19. God has given men one day of rest out of seven.

As Christians the Lord wants us to work, 1 Thessalonians 4.11, 2 Thessalonians 3.10-12. In the early church the Christians came together to worship on the first day of the week, Acts 20.7. This was the day when the Lord Jesus rose from the dead, John 20.1. However we do not have a **command** from the Lord to keep the first day of the week as a holy day, Galatians 4.10, Romans 14.5,6. Those who love the Lord will use the first day of the week for His glory. Certainly keeping the first day or the

113

seventh day or any day is not the way to be saved.

Of these seven feasts, on one, the day of atonement, people were to be sad, v.29. During the feast of trumpets they were filled with joy, v.40. The people were called together for these feasts by the sound of the silver trumpets, Numbers 10.2,10. However for the feast of trumpets, according to the old Jewish writers, a sheep's horn was used to call the people together. They could not do any hard work on the feast days, vs.7,8,21,25,35,36. On the sabbath and on the day of atonement, v.28, the people could not do any work at all. They could not even get their food ready, Exodus 16.23.

Most of the feasts of Jehovah also pointed forward to great events in Israel's later history.

1. The Passover, 23.5.

We saw complete rules for the Passover in Exodus 12. Here in Leviticus 23 we have the command given again in short form. For the Passover the people killed a perfect lamb. The blood saved the people from the judgment of God. The Passover looked forward to the death of our Lord Jesus Christ. Many years later our Saviour died on the day of the Passover, on the fourteenth day of the first month, Matthew 26.2.

2. Unleavened bread, 23.6-8.

The feast of unleavened bread came right after the Passover, from the fifteenth to the twenty-first day of the first month, vs.6-8. Complete rules for the feast of unleavened bread are also found in Exodus 12. Later, in Numbers 28.16-25 the Lord told Moses about the *sacrifices* to be made during the feast of unleavened bread.

The feast of unleavened bread followed the Passover. We have seen that bread without yeast speaks of what is pure and holy. The feast of unleavened bread speaks of the holy life which follows as a result of Christ's sacrifice. Bread also speaks of all of God's people as being one in His sight. For example on the gold table in the tabernacle the bread speaks of the twelve tribes of Israel, all one people in the sight of God. When we break bread at the Lord's Supper we show that we are all one in the Body of Christ, 1 Corinthians 10.16,17. So we can say that the feast of unleavened bread speaks of the holy life and the oneness of saints. Both of these things follow from the death of Christ.

3. The feast of first fruits, 23.9-14.

The people of Israel could not keep the feast of first fruits until later on when they had entered the land of promise. There are other commands in the book of Leviticus which look forward to the time when they would be living in the land of Canaan, 14.34; 19.23; 25.2.

The feast of first fruits was on the first day of the week, v.11. The people of Israel could bring a little of the first grain which they had cut. They must not eat any part of the new crop until they had brought the sacrifice to Jehovah, v.14. With the offering of first fruits they should also bring a lamb as a burnt offering, as well as a meal offering and a drink offering. The meal offering was twice as much as the meal offering of every day. More about the sacrifices of the feast of first fruits is found in Numbers 28.26-31.

With the grain they must bring a *drink* offering, v.13. God had commanded them to bring a drink offering with the daily burnt offering, Exodus 29.40,41. The laws about the sacrifices in Leviticus 1-7 say nothing about the drink offering. The people were to bring a drink offering with the meal offering, Numbers 6.17; 15.1-10.

The words *"the sabbath"* of verse 11 seem to mean the first sabbath after the crops were ready, Deuteronomy 16.9. This was usually in the first month of the year. It made the people of Israel remember that the harvest comes from God.

The feast of first fruits pointed forward to the time our Lord Jesus Christ rose from the dead. The Lord Jesus is the **first fruits** of those who died, 1 Corinthians 15.20,23. It is true that other people had been raised from the dead, for example, by Elijah and Elisha, 1 Kings 17.17-24 and 2 Kings 4.32-37. The Lord Jesus Himself raised at least three people from the dead, but these all had to die again. The Lord Jesus rose from the dead, never to die again. In the last days He will raise all the dead like a great harvest. He Himself is the first fruits of that harvest.

It will be a day of great joy for us when the Lord Jesus comes and raises all believers who have died, 1 Thessalonians 4.15-17. Many years later He will raise from the dead all other men who have ever lived. They must stand before God and go away to everlasting judgment, Revelation 20.12-15. It is our duty to tell them the way of salvation before it is too late.

4. The feast of weeks, 23.15—22.

The feast of weeks was held on the fiftieth day after the feast of first fruits. It was also on the first day of the week. In the New Testament this day was called Pentecost which means *"fiftieth"*.

For the feast of week's Israel offered a meal offering of new grain. They brought two loaves of bread for a wave offering, also a burnt offering (seven lambs, one bull and two rams with their meal offering and drink offerings). They also brought the sin offering (one goat), and a peace offering (two lambs). They must not do any hard work that day, but come together for a big meeting.

The wave offering for the feast of weeks was made with yeast, v.17. In this way it was different from the regular meal offering which was made without yeast, 2.11. We have seen that yeast speaks of evil and the meal offering is a picture of our Lord Jesus Christ. In Him was no evil whatever. The loaves of the feast of weeks make us think of the believer. Though not without sin we should present ourselves to God, Romans 12.1. We still have the old nature in us, but we belong to God. With the bread made with yeast Israel offered seven perfect lambs which speak of the Lord Jesus, v.18. All the other animals also speak of the sacrifice of the Lord.

The feast of weeks came at the end of the harvest when everyone had plenty of food. The Lord told His people to remember poor persons and strangers and give them some of their food, v.22.

The feast of weeks looked forward to the day of Pentecost. On that day believers in the Lord Jesus Christ were together in one place, Acts 2. Suddenly the Holy Spirit came on them and baptized them all into one Body, the Body of Christ. Since that day every believer has been given the Holy Spirit. *"Anyone who does not have the Spirit of Christ does not belong to Him,"* Romans 8.9. The Spirit of God has also brought us into the Body of Christ, 1 Corinthians 12.13.

Today we can know two wonderful facts: 1. A Man, after rising from the dead, is now seated in glory at God's right hand in heaven, Hebrews 8.1. 2. God the Holy Spirit lives in the hearts of believers on earth. The feast of first fruits and the feast of weeks are pictures of these two wonderful truths.

5. The feast of trumpets, 23.23-25.

The first three feasts of Jehovah were in the first month of the year. The feast of weeks was in the third month. The other three feasts were in the seventh month. The first of these three was the feast of trumpets on the first day of the seventh month. When the people heard the sound of the trumpets or rams' horns they came together. They did no hard work that day, but offered special sacrifices, Numbers 29.1-6. There were nine burnt offerings with their meal offerings and a young goat for a sin offering.

When the Lord comes for His people the sound of God's trumpet will be heard, 1 Thessalonians 4.16,17. The saints will be caught up to meet the Lord in the air. At that time the nation of Israel will begin to awake and many will seek the Lord. Today only a few Jewish people believe in the Lord. When the Church is taken out of the world, God will begin to deal with His people Israel once again, Romans 11.25.

6. The day of atonement, 23.26-32.

The day of atonement was on the tenth day of the seventh month. The high priest had special duties on the day of atonement, chapter 16. But the people were to do no work of any kind. They were to come together and "afflict" themselves, v.27. This means to be sorry for their sins. They were also to bring special offerings.

God strongly commanded the people to do no work at all on the day of atonement, 16.29; 23.28,30. The great lesson here is that we cannot work for our atonement. The work was completely finished by Another, the Lord Jesus Christ. The death of our Lord is seen in the sacrifices of the day of atonement, chapter 16.

The day of atonement also looked forward to the time when many true Israelites will be sorry for the great sin of their nation. God sent His Son into the world, but His own people would not receive Him, John 1.11. After the Church has been taken home to heaven many Jews will turn to Christ. At that time many people of Israel will indeed "afflict" themselves, Zechariah 12.10. At that time God will destroy those who do not repent, v.29. Those who repent will leave off their own works and put their trust in the Lord Jesus.

It is our joy to do this now in the day of His grace, Hebrews 4.10.

7. The feast of booths, 23.33-44.

We read of the seventh of the feasts of Jehovah, the feast of booths, in verses 33-36. All these seven feasts were times of special sacrifices, vs.37,38. The Lord told Israel what to do during the seven days of the feast of booths, vs.39-43.

Three times every year all the men of Israel were to come before the Lord, Exodus 23.14-16: the feast of unleavened bread, the feast of weeks and the feast of booths, Deuteronomy 16.16. The men had to come together at the place which God would choose. Later God chose Mount Zion in the city of Jerusalem, Psalm 132.13.

The day of atonement was a day of sorrow, but a short time after that, the feast of booths was a time of great joy, v.40. The people were to build little houses made of branches of trees. They lived in these little "booths" for seven days. The men were to come together on the fifteenth day of the seventh month and again on the twenty second day. They offered many sacrifices every day, Numbers 29.12-38.

The feast of booths reminded Israel that they lived in tents in the desert for many years after leaving the land of Egypt, v.43. The passover and the feast of unleavened bread also made the people think of great events in their history, Exodus 12.27,39.

The feast of booths was a time of great joy, v.40. It looked forward to the time when the Lord Jesus will rule in this world for 1000 years, Revelation 20.4,6. Then there will be great peace and plenty of food for all men in every country. People will remember the early days and hard times, but will praise the Lord for His goodness to them. We Christians will be in heaven with the Lord. We too will look back on the days of our lives in this world and praise God for His wonderful care over each one of us.

The people of Israel kept the feast of booths or tabernacles in 2 Chronicles 8.13, Ezra 3.4, and Nehemiah 8.13-18. In New Testament days the Jews still kept this feast, but not because they loved God. The Holy Spirit called it *"the Jews' feast"*, John 7.2. In the future when the Lord Jesus rules in this world, men of all nations will keep the feast of booths, Zechariah 14.16.

From this chapter we see that God commanded His people to keep the sabbath **every week** and seven feasts **every year**. Most of these feasts were in the first month or the seventh month. Five of the feasts were for one day only, but the other two lasted for a whole week each. The people could do no hard work on the first and seventh days of the feast of unleavened bread, vs.7,8. The same was true for the feast of first fruits, Numbers 28.26; the feast of weeks, Leviticus 23.21; the feast of trumpets, v.25. They could do no hard work on the first and last days of the feast of booths, vs.35,36. They could do no work of any kind on the day of atonement, but nothing is said about working on the passover day.

Some of these feasts look back to great events in the history of Israel. Most of them look forward to the future. The people of Israel could not understand the future meaning of the feasts, but we have the light of the New Testament. We can see how these feasts pointed forward to great events in God's plan for the nation.

FEASTS OF JEHOVAH

Month	Day	Feast	Past Meaning	Future Meaning
First	fourteenth	Passover	Saved in Egypt	Christ died
First	fifteenth	Unleavened Bread	Brought out of Egypt, Exodus 12.17	
First	sabbath	First fruits		Christ rose
Third	sabbath	Pentecost		Holy Spirit came
Seventh	first	Trumpets		The Lord will come for His Church and Israel will awaken
Seventh	tenth	Atonement	Israel will repent	
Seventh	fifteenth to twenty-second	Booths	Travelling through the desert	The Lord Jesus Christ will rule over the earth

For us there are no special days to praise and worship God. We gather together the first day of the week, the day of Christ's resurrection; but we can enter at all times into God's presence to praise and worship Him. He wants to hear us giving thanks to Him and glory to His Son.

Lesson 12
MORE INSTRUCTIONS, chapters 24-27.

The rest of the book of Leviticus has more rules which God gave to His people.

Oil and bread, 24.1-9.

We have seen God's commands for certain great days through the year. On these special days the people of Israel kept the feasts of Jehovah. For **daily** worship God commanded the people to bring pure olive oil, vs.1-4. It was Aaron's duty to keep the seven lamps in the gold lampstand burning at all times. Every morning and every evening Aaron and his sons had to look after the lamps.

God also told the people of Israel to prepare twelve loaves of bread for the gold table, vs.5-9. Every sabbath day Aaron set the bread in order in two lines of six loaves each. A little pure frankincense was put with the bread. Aaron and his sons ate the bread in a holy place.

We have seen commands about the oil and the bread before, Exodus 27.20,21; 25.30. Now the tabernacle has been built and God commanded the people to bring these things for their daily worship.

It is important that Christians should pray and praise the Lord every day. David and Daniel prayed three times each day, Psalm 55.17, Daniel 6.10. These are good examples for us.

A man spoke evil of Jehovah, 24.10-23.

Just at this time two men in Israel had a bitter quarrel. One of them was the son of an Egyptian. In the quarrel this man took the name of Jehovah in vain and broke the third command, Exodus 20.7. They brought the man to Moses and locked him up for the night, vs.10-12. It was important to know the will of God in this matter. If Israel wanted God's blessing they must judge this sin.

There was no sacrifice for such a sin. God showed Moses that this man would have to die, vs.13-16. All who heard the man should put their hands on his head. All the people threw heavy stones on him until he died, v.23. At this time the Lord gave again commands about sins of violence, vs.17-22.

Many men curse the name of the Lord today. It is very sad for a Christian when he has to listen to the terrible language of unsaved men. Why does not God judge them at once? We know that sin is just as bad today as it ever was. When the day of God's grace is over, He will surely judge all who reject Christ.

Years of rest, chapter 25.

God gave His people a day of rest every week. There were also special days of rest and a whole week of rest at the time of the feast of booths. This shows the grace of God because man has been commanded to work, Genesis 3.17-19.

God also gave Israel one year of rest out of every seven, Exodus 23.10,11. Now He told them not to plant their fields nor look after their vines. They could not even gather in the food which grew of itself. Men and animals, masters and servants, all should have a year of rest, 25.1-7.

Then after seven "weeks" of years, 49 years in all, there was a special year called the year of jubilee. This was another year of rest for all people in Israel. On the day of atonement in the seventh month of the fiftieth year a trumpet would sound through all the land. Then everyone was free to go back to his own home, vs.8-12.

Every man got his own land back again. If at any time during the 49 years a man of Israel became poor, he could sell his land. This would help him to pay his debts. He could only sell his land for the number of years which remained until the year of jubilee. The price of the land became less as the year of jubilee came near, vs. 13-17.

When Israel first entered the land of Canaan, they divided up the whole country and everyone got a piece of land. The law of the year of jubilee should have kept anyone in Israel from getting very rich or very poor. We never read that Israel kept this law. They did not even keep the law of rest in the seventh year. Because of this sin, after many years God gave Israel into the hands of the king of Babylon. They were prisoners in the land of Babylon for 70 years while the land had its rest. Read 2 Chronicles 36.21, Jeremiah 25.11, Daniel 9.2.

In the world today we see some people with great wealth and others who have nothing. This could not have happened in Israel IF God's law had been obeyed. The prophet Amos said that Jehovah would punish rich men in Israel because they sold poor people as slaves, Amos 2.6,7. James and Paul warned rich Christians to be kind to poor people, James 5.1-6, 1 Timothy 6.17-19. If we are rich we should be kind. If we are poor we should be satisfied with what we have. It is not our work as Christians today to try to help the poor by working for better laws. Our Lord and Saviour has told us very clearly to **preach the Gospel** to every creature. If rich or poor people accept Christ, they will be happy through all eternity. This is far more important.

The Lord promised Israel plenty to eat if they would obey His laws, vs.18-24. He would give His blessing in the sixth year so that the crops would be enough for *three* years. Israel should have believed this promise of God and obeyed His command to rest every seventh year.

If the man became poor and sold his property, a near relative could redeem it for him. The man himself could buy it back again if he became able to do so, vs.25-28. For example, Boaz, a near relative of Naomi, bought back the field which Naomi's husband had sold many years before, Ruth 4.1-10.

If a man sold his house in a city, he could redeem it any time within a year, vs.29,30. If he did not buy it back, after a year it would for ever belong to the person who bought it. However houses in villages could be redeemed at any time. Houses in villages were like the fields, they returned to the first owner in the year of jubilee, v.31. The Levites were not going to get any land and so their houses in the cities would come back to them in the year of jubilee, vs.32-34.

God commanded His people to be kind to one another. They should help the poor and not charge interest on money which they had lent to their brothers, vs.35-38. If a man of Israel sold himself as a slave, his master must treat him kindly. He would go out free again after six years, Exodus 21.2-4, or in the year of jubilee. The people of Israel belonged to Jehovah and He did not want them to be treated as common slaves, vs.39-46.

If a man of Israel sold himself as a slave to a *stranger,* he would go out free in the year of jubilee, vs.47-55. Even before that any relative in the poor man's family could redeem him. The price would depend on the number of years until the jubilee. If the jubilee was close at hand the price would be low. If there were many years yet to go, the price would be high.

There are two lessons for us in this chapter. 1. As sinners we have sold ourselves as slaves under the power of sin. Wicked king Ahab *sold* himself to do evil, 1 Kings 21.20,25. The year of jubilee is like the coming of the Lord. When the Lord comes, Satan's power over us will be at an end. Even now the Spirit helps us to gain the victory over sin in our lives. When the Lord Jesus Christ comes back, we will have new bodies and will not desire to sin any more.

2. In another way we can think of our property in this world becoming less valuable every year. When Christ comes, anything we own in this world will be without any value at all. We do not know when the Lord will come, so we should use everything we own for His glory and for His work. In this way we can save up riches in heaven, Matthew 6.20.

Blessing or curse, chapter 26.

The Lord was still speaking to Moses from Mount Sinai in chapter 26; see 7.38; 25.1 and 26.46. First He warned the people again not to make idols and commanded them to keep the sabbath, vs.1,2.

The rest of the chapter gives a list of blessings and curses. Israel would be *blessed* if they obeyed God's command. If they did not obey God would *punish* them.

If Israel obeyed God's orders and kept His commands He would send them rain, v.4, good crops, v.5, peace in the land, v.6, and victory over their enemies, vs.7,8. They would have plenty of children, v.9, and lots of food, v.10. Best of all, God would keep His covenant with them and live among them, vs.9,11. He would walk with them and be their God, vs.12,13.

God has not promised us as Christians that we would have peace and plenty in this world. We have been blessed with all spiritual gifts in heavenly places, Ephesians 1.3. God has promised us food and clothing, 1 Timothy 6.8, Matthew 6.25-34. We obey the Lord Jesus because we love Him, John 14.15.

It is sad to note that the bigger part of this chapter must be used to tell us about the *curses.* We read of five kinds of punishment, each one worse than the one before. 1. If they would not keep God's commands, He would send them sickness. Their enemies would gain the victory over them, vs.16,17.

2. If this did not bring them back to God, He would send a time of great hunger, vs.18-20.

3. If they kept on walking against God's will, He would send wild animals into the land, vs.21,22.

4. If they did not turn back to God, He would send war, sickness and more famine, vs.23-26.

5. If all this did not bring them back to God, He would punish them in great anger, vs.27-33. They would be so hungry they would eat their own children. He would destroy them *and* their idols also. Their enemies would come and take them away to far off lands.

While they were slaves in the country of their enemies, the *land* of Israel would have its sabbath, vs.34,35; 25.2. People who were left in the land would be filled with great fear, vs.36,37. People in the land of their enemies would not be happy, vs.38,39.

In these verses we see that God's punishment can be very painful. Still even when His people refused to obey, He would not completely forget His grace. If they confessed their sins, He would remember His covenant with Abraham, Isaac and Jacob, vs.40-45. He would not destroy the whole nation of Israel; He would leave at least a few.

The word if is found ten times in this chapter. In verses 3-13 we have the ifs of blessing. In verses 14-39 we have the ifs of judgment. In verses 40-45 the if of confession. As Christians we are blessed with all spiritual gifts, but we cannot enjoy these blessings unless we obey. "IF ye abide in Me and My words abide in you..." John 15.7.

Today the Father is teaching His children not to sin. He may let us get sick or send some other kind of trouble. When the Father is teaching us not to sin, it will certainly not be pleasant, but we can be sure that He loves us. In fact He wants to teach every son whom He loves. His plan is that we should share His holiness and bear the peaceful fruit of righteousness. In other words He wants us to be more like His Son, the Lord Jesus Christ, Hebrews 12.5-11. This is just another way that God uses to prove His wonderful love. He will not let us go on in sin because this would only bring us great sorrow later on.

Vows, chapter 27.

The last verse of chapter 26 describes the whole book of Leviticus. It does not mark the end of the book however because there is one more important subject, the matter of vows.

In time of trouble a believer in Israel might pray to Jehovah and make a promise. If the Lord would answer his prayer, he might promise to give himself or some of his property to the Lord. In some cases he could pay his vow in money. A priest had to decide on the value of the person who had been promised to the Lord, vs.1-8. The amount of money ranged from three pieces of silver to fifty. The amount depended on whether it was a man or a woman and on the person's age. If the man could not pay the full amount, the priest could use his own judgment and accept a smaller amount.

If a man promised to give one of his animals, he could not change it for another, vs.9-13. If it was an unclean animal it could not be used for a sacrifice. Then a priest would set a value on it. If the man wanted to redeem it he would have to pay the set amount *and* add one fifth more to it.

A man could promise to give a house to the Lord, vs.14,15, or a field, vs.16-25. The value of the field would depend on the number of years until the jubilee.

Every firstborn animal already belonged to Jehovah and a man could not give it to fill a promise. If a man had to die for some sin, no one could redeem him, vs.28,29.

One part in every ten belonged to Jehovah, vs.30-33. One tenth of the seed, one tenth of the fruit, every tenth animal was for God. You can read more about *"tithes"* in Deuteronomy 14.22-28.

In the New Testament we see that as Christians we belong to the Lord. **All** that I am and **all** that I have are given completely to the One who gave His all for me. We do not read about *vows* in the New Testament. *"For the love of Christ controls us because we are convinced that one has died for all; therefore all have died. And He died for all, that those who live might live no longer for themselves but for Him who for their sake died and was raised,"* 2 Corinthians 5.14,15. **"You are Christ's"**, 1 Corinthians 3.23.

The book of Leviticus tells us the rights and the duties of the priests and the Levites. This last chapter adds a little more. The priests had to decide on the value of anything which a man of Israel had promised. The people brought to the tabernacle of Jehovah the gifts which they had promised. These were for the priest and his family to eat.

THE TEACHING OF LEVITICUS

Paul told the young man Timothy to give time to *teaching,* 1 Timothy 4.13,16. What are the great truths which the Holy Spirit teaches us in the book of Leviticus?

About the Bible

One of the most important truths is that **God** has given us the Bible. Without this truth we could not be sure of any other teaching in the Bible. In Leviticus we read about 30 times that Jehovah *spoke* to Moses. We also see almost 30 times what the Lord *commanded* Moses. These words occur in almost every chapter of the book. We know from other verses that the whole Bible was given by God.

God

What does Leviticus teach about God Himself? As in Exodus, one important truth in Leviticus is that God is **supreme**. Many times He says *"I am Jehovah."* Because God is supreme, He has authority to tell men what to do.

The main truths about God in Leviticus are His **righteousness** and His **holiness**. We see God's righteousness, for example, in the commands of 19.35,36. Most of Leviticus has to do with the rules for sacrifices, priests and the tabernacle. It is very important that worshippers of God should worship according to God's Word. It is also important that they should live a clean life according to God's Word. Leviticus 17-20 gives many commands for the life of the people. We also see God's righteousness in chapter 26. God will surely bless those who obey Him and punish those who do not obey. We see that God is righteous in judging Nadab and Abihu at once, 10.1,2. He also judged the man who spoke evil of Jehovah, 24.14. Nadab and Abihu knew quite well what they were doing. This was very different from the sin of their brothers in the same chapter. The Lord accepted the sin offering of Eleazar and Ithamar, 10.16.

A small key can open the door of a big house. Sometimes one word, a **key** word, will help you to understand a whole book. A good key word for Leviticus is **holiness**. We see this in many ways. For example God showed His holy presence in the consuming fire, 9.24. The priests had to keep this fire burning on the altar at all times, 6.9,12. Only the high priest could come into the presence of God, the Most Holy Place, and only on the day of atonement. The many rules about the day of atonement teach the perfect holiness of God's presence. All Israel must be careful to eat only the flesh of *clean* animals, chapter 11. God would not forgive a sinner even if he did not know he was sinning. He had to bring a guilt offering. If a priest or leader made a mistake, his guilt offering must be greater than the offering of a common man. God **IS** holy.

Christ

The Lord Jesus Christ and His perfect work are brought before us in the pictures of Leviticus. Sacrifices speaking of Christ had to be perfect, *"without blemish"*, 1.3,10; 3.1,6; 4.3,23,28,32. 5.15, 18; 6.6; 9.2,3; 14.10; 22.19,20,21; 23.12,18. The meal offering was to be of fine flour with oil, frankincense, wine and salt, but no leaven or honey. These things speak of the perfect life of our Lord Jesus. He fulfilled God's Law perfectly. Christ gave Himself completely to God as in the burnt offering, 1.9.

The Lord Jesus Christ became a Man and so He could redeem men as One in the same family, 25.25,48, Hebrews 2.14. He took our sins on Himself and took them away to a far place, 16.10,22, Micah 7.19. His work on the cross makes it possible for us to feast on Him, our true Peace Offering, 7.15. We have peace with God through Christ, Romans 5.1. The life of the flesh is in the blood and the blood makes atonement for the soul, 17.11; Hebrews 9.14.

The feast of first fruits, 23.11, speaks of the resurrection of the Lord Jesus Christ who was the First Fruits from among the dead, 1 Corinthians 15.23. Aaron speaks of Christ in His present work as High Priest. Aaron was anointed with oil, 8.12; the Lord Jesus Christ was anointed by the Holy Spirit, Matthew 3.16. The Lord Jesus was different from Aaron; He never offered a sacrifice for Himself, 16.6; Hebrews 5.3; 7.27. The Lord Jesus entered into heaven in the value of His own blood, Hebrews 9.12. In many ways the book of Leviticus speaks of our Lord Jesus Christ.

Holy Spirit

Leviticus also has pictures of the Holy Spirit. Oil was put on the meal offering or mixed with it, 2.1,4. This speaks of the Holy Spirit working in and through the Perfect Man, the Lord Jesus. The anointing oil on the high priest speaks of the Holy Spirit. So does the olive oil in the gold lampstand which was burning brightly before the Lord at all times, 24.2,3. The feast of weeks looked forward to the day of Pentecost when the Holy Spirit came to live in God's people.

Sin

Leviticus teaches us something about sin. Sin is like leprosy inside a man. At first it is hidden, but sooner or later it becomes plain, chapter 13,14. The discharge of evil matter from a person's body is a picture of sin within, chapter 15. Sin can spread and make others unclean, 11.24; 13.45,46. The priest could tell if a man really had leprosy. In the same way it takes a spiritual man to see sin in another and help him, Galatians 6.1. If a man confesses his sin he can be made clean and brought back to God's people, 14.2,11.

Salvation

There are many different truths about salvation and Leviticus has pictures of some of these. A man sold as a slave could be redeemed by a near relative, but the sinner cannot redeem himself. When a man offered a sacrifice he put his hands on the animal's head, 1.4. This is like a sinner coming to Christ and believing in Him as the One who died for him. In chapter 16 on the day of atonement the sins of the nation were covered for another year.

127

This is a picture of the work of our Saviour which covers our sins forever, Hebrews 10.14. Anyone who understands the value of Christ's atonement can enter into rest. The sabbath day is a picture of God's rest. The peace offering satisfied God *and* the priest *and* the offerer. As Christians we have entered into a better rest, Hebrews 4.10, and we can feast with the risen Christ, Revelation 3.20.

The Church

The Old Testament does not teach the truth about the Church, but it does give us a few pictures. The twelve loaves of bread, Leviticus 24.5,6, speak of the people of God in their right order in His presence. The oil and the blood speak of the work of the Holy Spirit and of Christ. Both were put on the right ear, hand and foot of the priest. This showed that the whole man belongs to God. Priests must live a better life than the common people, 10.9, chapters 21,22.

Today all believers are priests of God. We can worship closer to God than Aaron and his sons did, but our lives must be better than the lives of others around us. Many people do things which they think are quite alright. The true worshipper of God must refuse to follow their example.

Future Things

The feast of trumpets in the seventh month is a picture of the coming of the Lord. Soon after the Lord comes, the people of Israel here on earth will be awakened. The saints in heaven will stand before the judgment seat of Christ. So in the seventh month on the day of atonement the people were sorry for their sins, but they were safe because of the blood. At the judgment seat of Christ the works of some will be burned up, but they themselves will be saved, 1 Corinthians 3.15. After the day of atonement the feast of tabernacles looked forward to the time when Christ will rule in this world for 1000 years. Then we will look back to the hard journey through the desert as a thing of the past. The year of jubilee also looked forward to the great day when men will be free from sin.

What a glorious day lies before us!
God's tomorrow is better than today.